SCARLET LETTER #4

The Mocking Serenade: Charivari and The Politics of Humiliation

by
Rod Dubey

Canadian Cataloguing in Publication Data
Dubey, Rod
The Mocking Serenade:
Charivari and The Politics of Humiliation

978-1-895166-38-5
1. Political Theory. I. Title
2. Cultural Theory.

Printed and bound in North America.

First published 2015

No Copyright

Published by Charivari
87 Franklin Street,
Uxbridge, ON L9P 1J5

Yes, there is beauty and there are the humiliated. Whatever difficulties the enterprise may present, I would like never to be unfaithful either to one or the other. But this still resembles an ethical code, and we live for something that goes farther than ethics. If we could only name it, what silence!

— *Albert Camus, Return to Tipasa*

Introduction

Charivari, Montréal (Québec), June 2, 2012,
photo by Benoit Rochon. Wikimedia Commons
The sign reads: "This is not a student strike. This is a society awakening."

> Old Abram Higback has been paying his good woman;
> But he neither paid her for what or for why,
> But he up with his fist, and blacked her eye.
> Now all ye old women, and old women kind,
> Get together, and be in a mind;
> Collar him, and take him to the shit-house,
> And shove him over head
>
> — A 19th C. hominy of Lincolnshire women in their charivari
> dealings with a wife beater[1]

Charivari is a centuries old ritual. Typically, it was a raucous serenade by townsfolk of a person or persons who had transgressed a local norm. Its aim was humiliation. Not infrequently, victims were accosted at night by a group of people in disguise, laughing, singing and banging pots and pans, or the victim might have been paraded through town, strapped to a chair.

The Mocking Serenade

Modern 'charivaris' (drawing from older versions in varying degrees) have been staged against governments and banks in recent years, in cities around the world: Madrid, Montréal, Santiago, Athens, and New York City, to name a few.

The fact that modern movements have adapted the charivari says something about the nature of their complaints. And what is also significant is the diversity of people who participate—old and young, radical and non-political, activists and some who never leave their front steps. They represent communities coming together in large numbers.

After the state radio station in Oaxaca was seized by local women in 2006, it was re-dubbed "Radio Cacerola" (Saucepan Radio), because of the use of charivari. Radio Cacerola gave voice to local people and supported the Asamblea Popular del Pueblo de Oaxaca (APPO) in the face of murderous retaliation by the state.

> The women behind the radio station do not appear to be militant fighters, but have most often been long-time residents who have finally become fed-up with their invisibility and maltreatment by successive state governments that have been promising to improve their lives for decades.[2]

In the face of a violent response, the "Kitchenware Revolution" in Iceland (their first 'revolution'), which followed the financial meltdown of 2008, brought down the conservative government.

> There were held several referenda to ask the citizens about paying or not the Icesave debt of their banks and, finally, a complex and unique process in which 25 common people of no political party were to be elected to form an Icelandic Constitutional Assembly that would write a new Constitution of Iceland.[3]

Many of the primary images of the charivari come from the 19th century British charivaris. As described by E.P. Thompson[4], they were a form of street theatre meant to humiliate and ridicule someone who had violated either a public or private local norm, a satire of public processions (inversions of state or military displays of loyalty and obedience, and so, a signalling that authority now resided with the public).

Often charivaris were staged to pass judgement on marriages (e.g. old man and young girl), so this has meant that they have often been seen only as reactionary. But the charivaris for public infractions were 'subversive,' according to Thompson. They were a form of self-rule. They were conducted by a community using play, noise and homemade arts to ridicule and reject certain actions of private or public individuals in defiance of the claims of official authority to be those who should make such determinations (the subjects of charivari could even be the clergy or judiciary, the passing of community judgement on official judgement). A subversive charivari was carried out not by those seeking power over others outside their community, nor was it a protest; it was people living by their own rules. Even the conservative charivari regarding a marriage was radical in that it was a challenge to the church and state which had condoned the marriage.

In broad terms, it might be said that European charivaris flourished through a period of great upheaval, when states secured their sovereign rule over communities, when common land was being enclosed and subsistence farming was being destroyed, when the Industrial Revolution was uprooting families, destroying communities and connections to the land, creating dependence, poverty and a new lower class of industrial workers within increasingly unlivable cities. It was an expansion of new and inter-related monopolies of power and the money economy, and of new formations of class. These were novel forms of humiliation, re-shaping social relations while destroying self-sufficiency, autonomy, and traditional identities.

The rural charivari was generally a festival of subsistence farmers—peasant families who marginally participated in larger economies, but were largely self-sufficient and autonomous—and/or townsfolk (craftsmen connected with the farming economy, whose role was dying with capitalism etc.). The charivari represented communities maintaining a degree of control. While conservative, perhaps religiously so, the charivaris around marriage were also about maintaining a form on independent life—family being central to the maintenance of a type of life; family as a collective of people with various skills who participated in running a farm.

Modern charivaris are sometimes not focused on particular policies so much as they are an attack on the dominant economic system bound up with political power. In Argentina, for example, the spontaneous charivaris of 2002 (its populous taking to the street chanting "They all must go!") disposed of several successive governments and initiated a series of local initiatives characterized by worker self-management and egalitarianism, by a barter system of millions operating outside of the official economy, by people suddenly confident in their own capacities. Economic, social and cultural dominance of individuals and communities, and the lack of alternatives, remain at the heart of modern humiliation and thus, modern charivari.

The subversive charivari (and related activities) are not only an inversion of legal order but are an inversion of the humiliation used by all forms of power that colonize, create poverty, and undermine independence. A charivari stakes a claim to the use of humiliation, refusing to be numbed by it, using it instead, as a means to control one's own cultural life.

The Mocking Serenade

Naomi Klein:

What made Argentina's 2001-02 uprising unique was that it wasn't directed at a particular political party or even at corruption in the abstract. The target was the dominant economic model—this was the first national revolt against contemporary deregulated capitalism.

It's taken a while, but from Iceland to Latvia, South Korea to Greece, the rest of the world is finally having its ¡Que se vayan todos! moment.

The stoic Icelandic matriarchs beating their pots flat even as their kids ransack the fridge for projectiles (eggs, sure, but yogurt?) echo the tactics made famous in Buenos Aires. So does the collective rage at elites who trashed a once thriving country and thought they could get away with it. As Gudrun Jonsdottir, a 36-year-old Icelandic office worker, put it: "I've just had enough of this whole thing. I don't trust the government, I don't trust the banks, I don't trust the political parties and I don't trust the IMF. We had a good country, and they ruined it."[5]

In the notes below I follow Raoul Vaneigem's view that spectacular society manufactures humiliation as generalized colonialism but I try to update this concept. I spend some time on charivari firstly because it is a ritual of contestation that inverts humiliation. The 'subversive' charivari, for public infractions seems to be the version that is often being currently revived, and this is an indication that what is being resisted with the modern use of charivari is not some specific political position but a challenge to the expansion of economic and political colonial power.

Close up of a sign decorating a defaced Alþingi (the parliamentary house of Iceland) in Reykjavík, reading, "For sale kr. 2,100.000.000" and "IMF Sold". 2009. photo by Jabbi

A SERENADE OF 'ROUGH MUSIC.'

From The Book of Days by Robert Chambers, 1832

1. A Brief Word on Charivari

Meanwhile Mr. Benjamin Grower, that prominent burgess of whom mention has been already made, hearing the din of cleavers, tongs, tambourines, kits, crouds, humstrums, serpents, rams'-horns, and other historical kinds of music as he sat indoors in the High Street, had put on his hat and gone out to learn the cause. He came to the corner above Farfrae's, and soon guessed the nature of the proceedings; for being a native of the town he had witnessed such rough jests before. His first move was to search hither and thither for the constables, there were two in the town, shrivelled men whom he ultimately found in hiding up an alley yet more shrivelled than usual, having some not ungrounded fears that they might be roughly handled if seen.

—Thomas Hardy, *The Mayor of Casterbridge*[6]

In an English skimmington (depicted in the image above, sometimes referred to as 'rough music'), an unwilling person (or their surrogate) who had violated a local norm, was noisily paraded through town in a satiric procession meant to humiliate them. According to E.P. Thompson,[7] these charivaris were accompanied by a raucous din (often the banging of pots and pans), laughter and "the mimicking of obscenities."[8] Verses (nominy) were a common part of the rituals, as was transvestism.

The skimmington was an English form of 'charivari,' an umbrella term for a centuries old tradition of rituals staged by members of a community and enacted against individuals who violated local norms. Operating in an extra-legal way, charivaris inverted legal order. In them, the community took it as their right to judge behaviour (including that of figures of authority), and enacted that right.

Competing aspects of 'community' were at work in a charivari. It represented a form of power over people (limiting one's personal freedom to deviate) but, at the same time, its actions were determined by its members, and it protected a certain level of autonomy against the imposition of external authority and codes. Charivaris didn't protect individual rights, in a modern way, but the collective right of a community to determine its distinctive culture and codes.

Roslyn M. Frank describes a form of charivari, the arrosa, a mock trial, in the Basque region. (Arrosas were meant to disgrace those who'd transgressed local norms.)

On the day designated for the celebration of the festival the villagers went about forming the tribunal and electing the people who were to play the principal roles in the mock trial, attempting to choose individuals for each role who were the most physically different from the person who they were going to imitate…

While the cast of characters was being chosen those who were to perform the role of the injured party and the accused were also designated. Here again the choice was dictated by the desire to find individuals who were comic counterparts, and they were attired in such a way that it was easy to see they were in fact caricatures. For example, the last recorded arrosa took place in Valcarlos, in 1930. It was organized because a young woman had been attacked by a young man. She called on her sister for aid and, since the latter was ironing at the time, she came with the hot iron in her hand and gave the attacker a blow with it, burning his face. In the mock trial the person playing the role of the attacker had the mark of the iron painted on his face. The actor was so ridiculous his very presence on stage made the audience burst into laughter.

After everyone was properly disguised the tribunal and the couple [actors] came in and took their places on the raised stage in the middle of the plaza. Along with the judicial authorities [actors] the village dancers came forward and, before the proceedings began they would execute a dance about the stage.[9]

Thompson noted that the variety of the forms and occasions of charivari makes generalizing about them difficult. Still, there were a number of frequent characteristics of charivaris in terms of form, context and function that are detailed in Thompson's essay.

- The rituals were satires, 'street theatre' that mocked state processionals and in doing so showed an acute familiarity with symbolism and an ability at inversion.
- They were outside of the legal process, policing transgressions that were often not covered by the law but which were deemed unacceptable by the community.
- The most successful charivaris worked because they reflected community wide feeling and the 'victim' was also a member of the community (so acutely felt the rejection and humiliation). In other words, they were the community acting on its own behalf.
- Charivaris were generally an alternative to violence against people; the mock ritual that humiliated someone perhaps being a means of displacing violence. They used humour and theatre instead. (But they were of serious intent. A mock public hanging, for example, signalled a real excommunication from the life of the community.)

A Brief Word on Charivari

Miniature du XIVe siècle représentant une scène de charivari,
Maître du Roman de Fauvel

- The values protected varied widely since they reflected local norms.

It should be noted too that the community power expressed was evanescent and did not devolve into some form of institutionalized rule. They did not establish a dedicated leader nor was their ambition power over other communities. The charivaris were not protest marches but a ritual theatre in which the community enacted a degree of (moral) autonomy.

The local norms that were violated, prompting a charivari, might be *domestic* infractions. These often reflected a patriarchal society according to Thompson (adultery, disapproval of certain marriages) but this category came to be dominated by the humiliation of wife beaters.

Or the occasion for charivaris might be *public* infractions. A strike-breaker could be humiliated, or a judge, official, policeman, preacher. Thompson argues that while domestic infractions were often judged in a conservative way, when the charivari was directed outward it was a subversive challenge to authority.

It is hard to disagree with E.P. Thompson when he notes having a problem with unqualified admiration of the charivari when the targets of charivaris could also be the outcast or the odd.

Commentators often wag their finger at the charivari as a form of barbarism, as a trampling of law and order, as aggressive and reactionary, concerned only with marriage. Often their sole focus is on charivaris that were met with violence. In spite of this, charivaris were typically not a form of barbarism but in marked contrast to the barbarism of external law and order, of a legal system that operated on behalf of a select few, that often had little correspondence to human decency, that pilloried people as a form of humiliation, jailed them for debt, and executed them for minor property offences. (And this is to say nothing of the activities of the state, which included mass slaughter in the forms of war, genocide and imperialism; state, economic power and war always being bound together.) Judges and lawmen were subject to charivaris for their inhuman verdicts.

Frank describes the arrosa as a form of mediation that restored peace between combatants and within a community, that mocked legal tribunals but didn't duplicate them — and even mocked mediators[10]. She argues that in the Basque region, the arrosas were a form of "social and political protest"[11] against the suppression of Basque norms. They were a rejection of assimilation and colonialism. Arrosas were "a political response to the incorporation of previously autonomous communities into state systems and the consequent process of class formation."[12]

In general terms, one can see certain charivaris as local responses to authority's exertion of its sovereignty and codes, destroying local norms and later, in rural areas, destroying subsistence farming as it supported the development of capitalism.

It could be argued that even 'conservative' charivaris (interventions into domestic affairs) were also 'subversive' insofar as they protected local culture and refused to accept the church and state as sole adjudicators over what was an acceptable marriage. Rejecting adultery, domestic fights, and marriages that undermined traditions were a form of cultural preservation (e.g. challenging the rich old man marrying a young girl was a challenge to the way in which class based wealth hindered the possibility of a young man finding a wife). Rurally, protecting the normative family was protecting the central component of a way of independent life. The family was central to self-sufficiency and subsistence farming, to operating a small farm, and to a realm where communities had a degree of autonomy.

Much has been made of the fact that the casserole dish and pots and pans come from the domestic sphere, suggesting a different perspective concerning women, but charivaris often maintained traditional patriarchal society according to Thompson. A woman who dominated her husband might be subject to charivari. On the other hand, women and girls were protected by charivaris where the law didn't. And women also staged their own charivaris. Casserole dishes might be said to reflect community since they were part of an ethics where bounty was shared among all members. They reflect the significance of everyday life, accessible objects to everyone, part of local culture, and of a community's norms rather than those imposed by hierarchical, masculine authority.

By the same token, the 'subversive' aspect of public charivari was actually conservative in protecting traditional society (e.g. against the church broadening which marriages it would accept). They were self-rule but still the enforcement of law and order. (An ethical society, A.N. Whitehead asserted, needs to be a stable society; the immoralities of war being the best exemplar of what happens when stability is destroyed.)

Charivari came to be used to shame and humiliate during political rebellions against the incursions of political power and industrialization. There are many historical records of charivaris meant to shame individuals working for the state, and against communities. (Charivaris were still staged by local communities, without central direction, even when part of the united efforts of farmers throughout a region.)

Dylan Thomas in *Rebecca's Daughters*:

> At the Pentre Arms, two small farmers are sitting, legs comfortably stretched out, in front of the bar room fire, with pipes and tankards. One is reading aloud, slowly, from a local newspaper, while his companion comments.
> '"Eighty gates in this county alone have been utterly destroyed".'
> 'It'll be eighty-three after tonight.'
> '"And a great number of tollhouses razed to the ground. In the neighbouring counties scarce a gate is standing..."'
> 'We'll beat them yet!'
> '"No-one can tell where Rebeccas will strike next. Authority is powerless".'
> 'There's a lovely ring that's got to it! "authority is powerless."'
> '"The destruction wrought by these ferocious scoundrels and incendiary rogues..."'
> 'Read that bit again, David Davies. Slowly!'[13]

The ceffyl pren was a Welsh version of rough music, aimed at humiliating violators of local norms. It came to be used in the Rebecca Riots, the rural insurrections of subsistence farmers against a political system of crippling tolls, hated

The Mocking Serenade

Official justice. The French highwayman Cartouche being publicly beaten to death, 1721

Official justice. In 16th C. Germany, Jews could be hung upside down between 2 dogs to further humiliate them as they were being executed,

A Brief Word on Charivari

Official justice. Hanging was a symbol of inversion so was associated with humiliation. One means by which Italian legal authority used humiliation was with the pittura infamant, government commissioned images of debtors, bankrupts and others to be hung in public places to humiliate them through symbolic upside down hanging. Debt is still characterized by a sort of shame that benefits economic normalcy. It is common for people to refuse to declare bankruptcy out of a sense of pride.

Poor Laws which were an attack on the poor, and even the Church of Wales. Participants ('Rebecca's Daughters') dressed as women and blackened their faces. Women's clothing was a means of anonymity, and inversion, and a symbol of a lack of leaders since Rebecca was the name of every participant.

Phil Carradice

> But why dress as women in order to carry out the raids? A traditional method of handing out social justice in Wales was to force the miscreant, whoever he might be, to ride through the streets on the ceffyl pren, a wooden horse. Blackened faces and cross dressing were part of the ritual, hiding the identity of those involved. Men dressing as women were seen to symbolise a world that had been turned upside down.[14]

E.P. Thompson:

> In the 1820s and 1830s in parts of South Wales the ceffyl pren was increasingly brought into use against 'public' offenders—in agrarian grievances, against prosecutors in cases of petty theft, against unpopular municipal officials, etc. The translation of the ritual from the private to the public domain was viewed by authorities with anxiety:
>
> "The right which is thus abrogated of judging...another man's domestic conduct, is certainly characteristic of a rude state of society; when the same measures are applied to...thwarting the operation of the laws of the land, they become of much more serious import. The principle is perfectly Irish, and...contains the germ of resistance to legal orders." ("First Report of the Constabulary Commissioners" 1839)
>
> This last observation was borne out by the use of the ceffyl pren in the 'Rebecca riots' against the turnpike tolls in South Wales in the 1840s. The 'Scotch Cattle' disturbances in the mining areas of the early 1820s (mainly in Monmouthshire) had already evinced ritualistic elements: Men, with blackened faces, dressed as women; animal-guising with horns, skins, and masks; the blowing of horns, lowing, rattling of chains, and firing of guns outside the homes of blacklegs or informers[15].

(Note: The reference to the 'Irish' nature of the riots, in the quote above, refers to the Whiteboys of Ireland, or Levellers, an agrarian group trying to protect subsistence farming, who attacked the infrastructure of agriculture—although they began non-violently by levelling ditches.)

A Brief Word on Charivari

Official punishment as Christian humiliation porn.
Master Francke, Saint Barbara Altarpiece panels Helsinki, before 1424
breast amputation and implied legal rape (a form of humiliation)

The Mocking Serenade

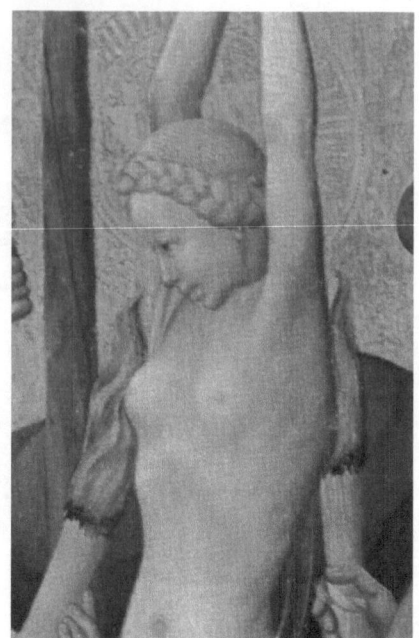

Official punishment as Christian humiliation porn.
Master Francke, Saint Barbara Altarpiece panels Helsinki, before 1424
hanging/burning (detail), by Meister Francke

Rebecca Riots (knocking down a toll gate), Illustrated London

There were even aspects of charivari that found their way into the activities of the Luddites. Luddite activity was often in the Levellers' vein, smashing the looms and machinery of mass production that displaced skilled craftspeople. (Their actions are often referred to as 'violence' although it was property destruction. Violence—meaning, to hurt people—was/is a favoured tactic of the state.) Less famously, the Luddites (small textile artisans in a society of subsistence farmers) played Robin Hood, demanding money at night, in disguise, (becoming mummers), to give to the victims of the new poverty. Similarly, charivaris often demanded a fine of wealthy newlyweds that would be given to the poor. Other Luddite activities showed a kinship to charivari as well; such things as cross-dressing and the use of noise (customarily yells) as a weapon. ("The yell was a long one, and when it ceased, the night was yet full of the swaying and murmuring of a crowd." Charlotte Bronte, *Shirley*)

In "Ned Ludd's Mummers Play," Norman Simms argues that the Luddites were in the same folkloric tradition as the charivari:

> Ned Ludd was the mythical centre of the revolt, and in each area of discontent the leading individual would act in the name or in the disguise of Captain Ludd. He could have clerks, lawyers, friends, wives, sons, and enemies, and yet what the Luddites did was 'to lud' [elsewhere Simms states that this might derive from the Latin word 'ludos,' for game or play, although he also gives other possibilities], to do something more than merely break machines or run amok through

Lady Ludd

the streets and lanes of north England. They were performing some form of juridic folk play, the mumming of Ned Ludd."[16]

In Simms' view, these groups sought to resist external control and the juridic use of violence against them (by comparison, Luddites were often executed by the state) by taking communal juridic power in a satiric way and directing a folk response.

The Luddites were the most modern of groups, in many ways, in attacking the trajectory of the development of technology (rather than the idea of technology per se) that facilitated mass production and monopoly economic control, stripping individuals of skills and autonomy, making them 'poor' and an underclass because of it, their communities decimated and humiliated, disposed people migrating to the city as unskilled labour. In challenging the emerging capitalism, they challenged the seeds of modern alienation and wage labour. The Luddites also directed themselves at an industry flourishing due to slavery (from the mass production of cotton from slave holding America that was the outcome of the cotton gin, a change which also crippled the Indian economy). Mass production always leads to oppression (e.g. the fashion industry is still characterized by exploited labour in other countries). Anywhere there is colonialism and consumerism there is slave, or near slave, labour (e.g. sugar production, minerals for computers/cell phones, etc.).

The Luddites end goal was the same as what was protected with subversive charivari; economic independence and local control.

Rituals like the arrosa were an inversion of people's typical experience of humiliation, which was something used against them, to enforce authority over them. Instead, humiliation became a means to protect autonomous culture.

Evelin Lindner:

> The research on humiliation that I carried out documents myriads of ways in which hierarchical systems of domination/submission have been held in place by routine humiliation throughout the past ten thousand years… Slavery, bondage, serfdom, feudalism, lords, vassals, Apartheid, Coverture — terms abound that describe the various degrees to which a person could lose the relative sovereignty a hunter-gatherer enjoyed prior to ten thousand years ago, and the different ways in which a person could be subordinated, stripped of her rights, and turned into the property of her master.[17]

Lindner points out that people are brought up to believe that humiliation is the natural order of things and not really humiliation at all. The powerful, however, retain the (exclusive) right to feel humiliation.

A Brief Word on Charivari

It is not specific rituals—such as placing people who steal a loaf of bread in a pillory for public humiliation—that is the basis of the humiliation inflicted by power, although any display of brute force is significant. The pillory was just one example of how authority can control people and define any activity as shameful and illegal which threatens the order of the society over which they rule. All forms of power humiliate because their rule consists in asserting and enforcing their own codes, destroying self-sufficiency and autonomy, infantilizing and creating dependency, and therefore, sabotaging human dignity. What was happening in Europe, since the 16th century, was part of a long history of inequality and enslavement.

Many of Us Will Have to Get at It—It Will Do Us Good.

George Herriman, 1907

1903, Dukhobor nudity began as a part of religious worship but was used during conflicts with authorities as a way to defy authority through an insistence on their own autonomy; refusing Western notions of shame was tantamount to living their own culture.

2. Some Words of Definition

I should clarify my use of the terms humiliation and shame—not from some claim to expertise but because they have no fixed meaning.

I follow the distinction made by Avishai Margalit who speaks of 'normative humiliation' and 'psychological humiliation.'[18] Slavery is normative humiliation. You have degraded the person. Yet the slave may retain his/her dignity and not feel psychologically humiliated. It is in this way that a society can humiliate people without its subjects feeling humiliated.

And, oppositely, a person can feel psychologically humiliated although the normative conditions for it don't exist (e.g. if one's socks don't match). One can feel humiliation, assuming that others are looking at them negatively, even if it is not the case. Psychological humiliation only requires that someone thinks they are being humiliated.

Power attempts to induce people to feel humiliation for behaviour that threatens its concerns (e.g. the bankrupt or draft dodger) or uses humiliation to consolidate its power. For example, our sense of humiliation can be manipulated to link our identity with some group and its leaders. ('Germany has been humiliated by Jews so we must respond in kind').

Humiliation consists of losing yourself, of becoming the other and adopting a negative perspective of yourself, such as happens with colonialism where you become a 'savage' or 'poor' and accept this as self-description. (Normative humiliation combined with psychological humiliation in the case of poverty.) We accept hierarchy and debasement. It is a public act because it concerns itself with the judgement of the other (in fact or imagination).

Howard Zinn recounts the story of a Dukhobor who refused military service in 1917. He was tortured to death and placed in a coffin dressed in a military uniform to "humiliate his family." The humiliation consisted in a reconstruction of the man's identity to be that of a soldier; the ability to control identity being central to the ability to humiliate.[19]

Shame is sometimes used as a synonym for humiliation and in these cases I find that it can either accord with how I use humiliation or how I use shame. Milan Kundera in *Immortality*:

> The basis of shame is not some personal mistake of ours, but the ignominy, the humiliation we feel that we must be what we are without any choice in the matter, and that this humiliation is seen by everyone.

Shame, as I use it, is also a failure to meet a particular standard and is sometimes played out in public, sometimes being forced upon us, but I generally use shame to refer to moral issues, as an extreme form of guilt where we condemn ourselves for moral failures. It therefore can have an invisibility because it is the failure to meet personal ethical demands that go to the heart of our identity (e.g. we laugh along at something despicable but once alone feel shame for it, our values revealing themselves only to ourselves).

Religion attempts to give shame a public face in order to shape it. God is defined as he who is able to see what is hidden. We are encouraged to reveal ourselves and admit shame. We are crippled by shame as 'sinners,' a vile designation shredding all sense of self-esteem, and then need forgiveness from a celestial third party, obtained through chosen humiliation. Psychoanalysis later emerges as a consumer item operating on much the same basis. Shame is only overcome by relinquishing privacy and control.

Religion, of course, not only attempts to determine when we should feel shame but demands obedience and ascribes value to the humiliation of subservience. St. Thomas:

> The virtue of humility consists in keeping oneself within one's own bounds, not reaching out to things above one, but submitting to one's superior. (Summa Contra Gent., bk. IV, ch. lv, tr. Rickaby).

All forms of power ascribe shame to behaviour that undermines them: quitting school, being unemployed, squatting, disobeying God, etc. Heteronomous (in the Kantian sense) morality. With the charivari, villages rejected official morality and laws that did not agree with local norms.

The charivari illuminated hidden acts, not thoughts. It announced, in fact it shouted out infractions. 'We know you beat your child and everyone for miles around now knows it as well! Feel shame!' Charivaris were frequently conducted at night, with the nighttime morality that characteristically inverts the daytime morality of authority. Blazing fire and noise uniting it with every aesthetic and personal impulse that seeks to manifest another sort of moral reality away from the restraints of the day-to-day controlled environment of family, church and state.

In *Sex at Dawn*, authors Ryan and Jethá see the fight over who controls and defines shame and humiliation not only as central to sexuality (their primary concern) but as central to the administration and control of resources within a community (i.e. both domestically and publicly). For example, while speaking of the Chinese Mosuo — a matriarchal society with no marriage, where a woman and her kids live in her mother's house and men merely visit women — they write:

> Mosuo women and men unashamedly report having had hundreds of relationships. Shame, from their perspective, would be the proper response to promises of or demands for fidelity. A vow of fidelity would

be considered inappropriate—an attempt at negotiation or exchange. Openly expressed jealousy, for the Mosuo, is considered aggressive in its implied intrusion upon the sacred autonomy of another person, and is thus met with ridicule and shame.[20]

The Mosuo can obviously feel jealous and possessive, as we all can, but to demand that someone limit their autonomy because of it is seen as coercive. When shame is defined by a community, insisting on its own codes, it can also be that which undermines autonomy and unique culture. For example, Ryan and Jethá argue against Hobbesian inspired theories of *homo economicus*—assertions that humans will always strive for economic power—arguing that, in the past, small groups of people maintained equal use of the commons through shaming. Locals would have shamed someone who obtained more sheep, they assert, attempting to take more than their share of available resources. Shame protected communities from challenges to individual freedom and self-sufficiency without the use of violence. Ryan and Jethá argue that when groups moved beyond a certain size, that the intense scrutiny of the actions of people by their neighbours disappeared. Not only was the commons lost when this happened but it was ecologically destroyed by greed. "What allows these chain-linked tragedies is the absence of personal local shame."[21]

The absence of this sort of 'personal local shame' (e.g. driving huge, gas-sucking SUVs) is a central feature of modern life.

Jews humiliated in a charivari type parade

Jules Arsène Garnier, Le supplice des adultères

3. The Ugly Charivari

Because psychological humiliation does not require a state of normative humiliation, what we feel to be humiliation can be manipulated and co-opted in ways that increase the authority of particular leaders who articulate an apparent sense of shared humiliation (e.g. 'Islam has been shamed!'). The resulting rituals of humiliation are always about increasing the power of the few and in the end, they increase the general humiliation rather than alleviate it because normative humiliation (as the loss of autonomy and personal freedom) is increased.

Hitler, an oft cited example, argued for a war, in part, to reverse 'Germany's humiliation' when the peace after WWI was signed. Invoking these feelings fuelled acceptance for his imperialistic ambitions and (the connected) rabid antisemitism. Propagandizing about humiliation served to override personal moral responsibility; social upheaval leading to the suspension of ethical norms.

The charivari is a vocabulary of forms that are open to all, to a state, or to any group wishing to obtain power through the use of humiliation. In itself it is neither politically radical nor reactionary, not necessarily a force for good or for evil. Like all rebellion, it can be a means to establish autonomy or enslavement, so can support the reign of any large group or wannabe dictator. The so-called enemy might be the West, or Jews, or the aristocracy, or black men who speak to white women.

What distinguished 'subversive' charivaris (although all charivari is, arguably, subversive) in their use in protecting community norms, or in their support of rebellion against imposed authority, was that they shared the qualities of being managed by a community, were opposed to authority, did not install leaders, were evanescent, were an alternative to physically violent responses, and were non-ideological.

Oppositely, charivaris can be an extension of a state's war machine. The humiliation of female 'collaborators' after WWII, a case in point, was particularly coloured by religious notions of shame (photos of these charivaris are reminiscent of Jules Arsène Garnier's "Le supplice des adultères").

According to Antony Beevor in "An Ugly Carnival," these acts were not a reflection of the broader community:

> It may seem strange that head-shaving, essentially a rightwing phenomenon, should have become so widespread during the leftist liberation euphoria in France in 1944. But many of the tondeurs, the head-shavers, were not members of the resistance. Quite a few had been petty collaborators themselves, and sought to divert attention from their own lack of resistance credentials. Yet resistance groups

Paris, 1944, German Federal Archives, Wikimedia Commons

could also be merciless towards women. In Brittany it is said that a third of those civilians killed in reprisals were women. And threats of head-shaving had been made in the resistance underground press since 1941.[22]

These acts were an outcome of a state war and mass nationalism. They were either the acts of impotent, individual cowards, or acts — often of murder, following through on threats meant to help defeat the enemy — by quasi-state groups. The cowardly violence against women was a response to the humiliation of occupation, military defeat, and to men's humiliating loss of 'their' women to German soldiers. According to Beevor:

> Many French people as well as allied troops were sickened by the treatment meted out to these women accused of collaboration horizontale with German soldiers.

(I assume that a fear of being seen as disloyal or traitorous caused many people to be silent.)

The actors were blind to the collaborators, as real people. (The size of a community, as per Ryan and Jethá, matters, since a large community increases individual anonymity.) 'Guilt' was divined by ideology, not from the familiarity that could have only come in small communities. It didn't matter if the women who 'collaborated' had been raped, coerced, motivated by desperation to feed their children, prostitutes, Jews seeking to avoid the holocaust, or innocent of the charges. They were all guilty within the simplistic polarity between the fluid determinations of good and evil that are stirred by war and religion. A scapegoat

The Ugly Charivari

was needed, guilty or not. Women had their heads shaved, sometimes marked with swastikas to signal them as transgressors (with Biblical resonances, fittingly, because that is also where the practice of head shaving began, according to Beevor).

At the same time, the transgressors could be paraded naked to humiliate them (the original Biblical shame), stripping them of the clothing which is a critical part of the expression of individual sexuality and identity, signalling that the women's sexuality was now under the control of the mob. Since sex and love, uncontrolled by authority, are always the ultimate crimes of sedition, these women were repossessed as a spoil of war (the opposite of the cross-dressing and sexuality evident at times in old radical charivaris) to make up for the perceived humiliation of the past by administering humiliation.

Antony Beevor:

> Revenge on women represented a form of expiation for the frustrations and sense of impotence among males humiliated by their country's occupation. One could almost say that it was the equivalent of rape by the victor.

The photos from Abu Ghraib prison in Iraq are just the latest incarnation of the use of humiliation and shame as a weapon of war; reflections of the ability of the state to inflict humiliation to maintain its power. (Officially frowned on by the state when it does not officially do the humiliating itself, such as is done in Guantánamo Bay Prison.)[23]

Humiliation ritual here is an auto-da-fé. It justifies a lack of ethical integrity because of loyalty to the aims of a larger group, and that group's supposed

Nov. 28, 2003, US Army SSG Ivan Frederick sitting on an Iraqi prisoner

'humiliation.' It is fostered by the anonymity of the large group where personal responsibility can be disowned. This brings to mind Donal McGraith's *The Wild and the Free*[24] which argues that a primary outcome of the emergence of groups (coincident with the end of the relative autonomy and happiness of prehistory) was the effect of creating loyalties which frustrated the possibility of individuals acting ethically. Loyalty to groups demands compliance to its interests and equates this with the ethical.

If groups, such as community and family, are a means of mutual protection, this understandably prioritizes loyalty. But, in keeping with McGraith, one could argue that 19th century charivari was not about supporting loyalty per se — members of the community could be rebuked — but in enforcing local moral codes rather than the codes of a new sovereignty (who made loyalty the primary ethical value, and appealed to it to have people act against their local self-interest).

The charivari in North America often devolved into shivarees and celebrations of marriage — think tin cans tied to the back bumpers of cars. According to Pauline Greenhill,[25] writing about new world charivaris, they became gang-like larks by young men who marched up to the home of newlyweds to coerce food and drink for themselves in a fun-loving lark (except when an attack on difference; mixed racial marriages, for example, would be aggressively shivareed by angry young men, gang manifestations always being consistent with enforced loyalty. The 'other' is the enemy.) Even the noise shifted from 'feminine' pots and pans to masculine music.[26] The point seems to have been to demand drinking money (followed by handshakes and good wishes all around) rather than to change behaviour. Greenhill argues that one evident reason that charivaris changed to affirmation from condemnation was an obvious shift in the nature of communities. Farmers had become small business people, were colonized, and no longer subsistence farmers. "Politically and socially, individual farm ownership meant conservative values."[27]

Writers such as Dominique Moïsi have pointed to the very real presence of humiliation in the Arab world that is a product of such factors as U.S. imperialism and their overthrow of regional governments, the ability of Israel to act with impunity, and the dominance of Western cultural products. Moïsi points to the ability of marginal terrorist groups (as with other authoritarian groups) to use humiliation to enhance their authority and agenda. He describes this humiliation in *The Geopolitics of Emotion*:

> Humiliation is impotence, an emotion that stems above all from the feeling that you are no longer in control of your life either collectively, as a people, a nation, or a religious community, or individually, as a single person. Humiliation peaks when you are convinced that the Other has intruded into the private realm of your own life and

made you utterly dependent. Humiliation encapsulates a sense of dispossession toward the present and even more so toward the future, a future in utter contrast with an idealized, glorified past, a future in which your political, economic, social, cultural conditions are dictated by the other.[28]

This sounds reasonable, since all colonized people have likely felt this, but what can happen when there is a collective humiliation is that authoritarian groups emerge. They co-opt humiliation, use it as self-justification for their group and their leadership, and demand loyalty. I suspect that the sense of impotence that is the outcome of imperialism may be the reason the individual feels powerless. (Communities staging charivaris were empowered.)

The increase in foreign recruits to Islamic terrorist groups is possibly because of people's (in their own countries) individual experiences of humiliation through things like racism and the inability to assimilate or gain opportunities. These people cleave to a group based on identity because it seems to offer power against humiliation (since, arguably, protection is the reason for all social groups that cease to be inclusive of shared autonomy).

To some degree, Islamic terrorism is also a variation of the way in which religion draws upon humiliation. The humiliation one feels individually is seen as an insult to Christianity or Islam. One suffers the humiliation of being stripped of even the autonomy of one's own feelings.

The tendency of any large scale resistance always carries a similarly possible loss of autonomy, towards personal subservience to state, religion or class. Even a workers' revolution develops leaders who, we are told, are only a temporary expediency, but which always become a new, entrenched power (that humiliates the individual). One cannot achieve autonomy through leaders. Charivari can be a part of revolution but forms of charivari like the arrosa are only consistent with leaderless, anti-authoritarian efforts at autonomy.

Photo by Nickolas Muray, 1932

4. On the Nature of Modern Humiliation

Humiliation is sometimes discounted as insignificant, described as something that haunts us, but only over frivolous matters. William Ian Miller, for example:

> The fear of humiliation is the fear that causes people to feel greater mortification for being discovered violating norms of body control and decorousness (e.g. passing gas) than for offending against more serious moral and legal norms (cheating on income tax, stealing from the workplace, adultery, betrayal). Shame occupies itself with the big, the moral, the religious; humiliation tends to be grounded more trivially, engaging the conventional and decorous.[29]

Miller goes on to analyze the day-to-day occurrences of humiliation. No attempt is made to connect instances of humiliation, as he labels them, with social conditions. Yet in spite of himself, many of Miller's examples reflect the 'political' nature of humiliation; of how it is tied to class and etiquette, for example. A person who uses humiliation to put down another, might be a person wishing to elevate their social status by diminishing the other, or someone simply trying to level the playing field by bringing a pretentious person down.

Arguably—to take the opposite approach to Miller—humiliation is at the heart of life today. And it is exactly that which seems trivial which is most significant.

Jean-Jacques Rousseau, wrote in *The Social Contract*,

> Whoever sang or danced best, whoever was the handsomest, the strongest, the most dexterous, or the most eloquent, came to be of most consideration; and this was the first step towards inequality, and at the same time towards vice. From these first distinctions arose on the one side vanity and contempt and on the other shame and envy: and the fermentation caused by these new leavens ended by producing combinations fatal to innocence and happiness.[30]

I buy a cheap car to get me from A to B. I think that I am above conspicuous consumption yet when I hear two people sniggering about my rust bucket I feel humiliated. This is an abasement of self. I have stood outside myself, seen myself through the eyes of the other, and embraced their values over my own. I have negated myself and become other (as I imagine them).

The Mocking Serenade

This is how consumerism works, as Raoul Vaneigem has pointed out. He appears to draw from Rousseau who defined the feelings of being ruled as "shame and envy" (a good summary of modern life) and here envy becomes humiliation:

> The feeling of humiliation is nothing but the feeling of being an object ... It is a belief in the happiness of others, an inexhaustible source of envy and jealousy which gives us a vicarious feeling of existence. I envy, therefore I am. To define oneself by reference to others is to perceive oneself as other. And the other is always object. Thus life is measured in degrees of assimilation. The more you choose your own humiliation, the more you 'live': the more you live the orderly life of things.[31]

Consumer humiliation points to the failure to challenge the dominant economic structure as the primary source of shame in the modern world.

Vaneigem is not defining humiliation as an outcome of being looked at per se, but of adopting the viewpoint of the other, and of wishing to remake ourselves because of a belief that we are lacking. This is colonialism. Ultimately, he applies the concepts of colonialism and assimilation to all of modern life.

Colonialism undermines the sustaining traditions and norms of a culture (that which charivari protects), devaluing them and replacing them with a belief in the values of the culture of the other. The colonized then destroy their own culture while trying to attain the new.

A case in point, for clarification. (This is a limited instance of colonialism meant to show the relationship to consumerism and the triumph of the economic model, of a dollar and cents evaluation over all of life. In many locales, colonizers also steal land and resources, slaughter, and enslave. To paraphrase Mark Twain in *Following the Equator*, between 'robbery, humiliation and murder' the white man's claim that he is better than how he describes 'the savage' is a humourous assertion.) For the last two winters in Canada we have seen numerous media stories of native people in Northern Ontario suffering because of the absence of 'adequate housing.' People are living in uninsulated shacks, in some cases during

On the Nature of Modern Humiliation

Photograph of students from Fort Albany Residential School reading in class overseen by a nun c 1945.

the middle of winter. Yet this is a people who have lived for thousands of years in these conditions and developed unique forms of shelter. These forms are no longer acceptable. Colonialism has made the locals poor and in need of 'housing.' Poverty is the triumph of a particular economic model, and of the replacement of autonomous culture with a need for specific commodities (housing, education, religion, healthcare, policing).

Traditional methods of shelter are no longer an option. They have been branded as substandard, in the general re-evaluation of native cultures by the standards of the immigrant culture.

Every aspect of traditional native life in these areas was undermined by colonialism; from being seen through the prism of white values. The lack of schools meant people were 'ignorant.' Lack of Christianity meant they were 'savages,' and so on. All needs, whether it was shelter, learning, healing, were translated into a 'need' for something that could be consumed to overcome it (development).

The lack of these commodities means that these people are now poor. They have become infantilized, dependant, and humiliated in a society of despair, with one of the highest suicide rates in the world. When people shiver in shacks the only response open to them is to humiliate the government through a media spectacle until they come in to build houses.

Residential schools, where children were beaten for using their own language, were a part of cultural genocide. The aim was to 'assimilate' natives into white society, meaning that they will have lost all traditional values. And this persists. The current assimilation tactic of the Canadian government is to push for their own version of enclosure; the privatization of shared native land into individual plots meted out to members. This will supposedly allow individuals to borrow money to start businesses and assimilate into the economic mainstream. Many will undoubtedly sell their houses (and perhaps fund a move to a city somewhere) which will effectively destroy the local land base as it is taken over by outsiders.

A respectful approach to native culture would have been silence from the outsiders, to learn from it, but white culture steamrolls in its loudness. The essential thing that was lost in the north was not just the traditional forms of shelter, but the cultural independence to determine one's own needs, replaced by commodity culture.

Reclaiming past independence is not the same as 'native control' or 'native sovereignty' over 'native nations.' These are political initiatives as stated by Western style native politicians re-envisioning their past in Western terms, and longing for a future with Western style political organizations, with Western style nationalism and the linking of humiliation under the leadership of another. (Even though this type of leadership is encouraged by the dominant culture, since it recognizes no other form, it is still about authority coming to rest within a political institution and not with individuals.)

What the critique of colonialism has done is to obscure the fact that all modern culture is alike, that we are all colonized, and it mitigates against the possibility that we might form alliances not based on race, nationality, and identities, but on shared experience. What Vaneigem's thoughts on humiliation suggest is that the critique of colonialism is no longer valid as the critique of the history and future of imperial subjects because it separates people into an us and a them. Northern communities followed a similar trajectory to elsewhere in the West when people lost the means and skills to be self-sufficient as a result of the industrial revolution. Real suffering ensued from depredation when self-sufficiency became impossible. People were humiliated by being stripped of the means to be independent, by adopting the values of authority, by becoming infantilized and dependant, and losing the ability to think that any sort of option outside of the dominant economy and culture was possible.

And poverty is also a moral judgement. It is to designate a group as being in need of care. Incarceration and later, care, established superiority over the 'poor.'

Of course, the social use of the concept of poverty justifies the transfer of tax money to the wealthiest, in the systemic propping up of an economic structure that supports monopoly; where political and economic power rest in the same hands.

On the Nature of Modern Humiliation

Hell's Kitchen, Manhattan, NYC, by Danny Lyon
Photo caption by the author: "The wall painting reads: 'The neighbourhood belongs to the people not big business'. The inner city today is an absolute contradiction to the main stream America of gas stations, expressways, shopping centers and tract homes. It is populated by blacks, Latins and white poor."

Privatization is an important manifestation of this practice, and the outsourcing of care and incarceration are economically critical to the survival of modern capitalism.

Of the current state of affairs, in Britain, Seumas Milne writes:

> Privatisation isn't working. We were promised a shareholding democracy, competition, falling costs and better services. A generation on, most people's experience has been the opposite. From energy to water, rail to public services, the reality has been private monopolies, perverse subsidies, exorbitant prices, woeful under-investment, profiteering and corporate capture.
>
> Private cartels run rings round the regulators. Consumers and politicians are bamboozled by commercial secrecy and contractual complexity. Workforces have their pay and conditions slashed. Control of essential services has not only passed to corporate giants based overseas, but those companies are themselves often state-owned — they're just owned by another state.

The Mocking Serenade

U.K. satire, 1926
Caption: "The Subsidised Mineowner - Poor Beggar!"

Report after report has shown privatised services to be more expensive and inefficient than their publicly owned counterparts. It's scarcely surprising that a large majority of the public, who have never supported a single privatisation, neither trust the privateers nor want them running their services.

But regardless of the evidence, the caravan goes on.[32]

Natives maintain social value as savages, as a resource to exploit and demonize, as a moral lesson of what to avoid and which values to embrace.
Gerald Vizenor:

The indian is a daemon, a modernist simulation of the other in the wicked cause of savagism and civilization.[33]

Native or white, we are all shaped by colonialism, which destroys the possibility of self-sufficiency and makes us subjects living according to values and ideology that are preached to us, inculcated in schools and mass media, while we attempt to consume beyond necessities in order to avoid humiliation, and to make all human striving measurable in economic terms. The question of tactics about how to achieve independence from this cycle emerges.
Vaneigem again:

From the moment when the collapse of colonial power revealed the colonialism inherent in all power over men, the problems of race and colour become about as important as crossword puzzles ... Human relationships can hardly be discussed in terms of more or less tolerable conditions, more or less admissible indignities. Qualification is irrelevant. Do insults like 'wog' or 'nigger' hurt more than a word of command?... Yesterday's anti-colonialists are trying to humanize today's generalized colonialism. They become its watchdogs in the cleverest way: by barking at all the after-effects of past inhumanity.³⁴

(Vaneigem can dismiss qualifications, like "problems of race and colour," and while this may be true with psychological humiliation, there can still be different degrees of normative humiliation. The slave suffers from a degree of normative humiliation that the rest of us don't.)

Jean Baudrillard:

> It is very naive to look for ethnology in the Savages or in some Third World—it is here, everywhere, in the metropolises, in the White community, in a world completely catalogued and analyzed, then *artificially resurrected under the auspices of the real*, in a world of simulation, of the hallucination of truth, of the blackmail of the real, of the murder of every symbolic form and of its hysterical, historical retrospection—a murder of which the Savages, noblesse oblige, were the first victims, but that for a long time has extended to all Western societies.³⁵

In its stark outlines, Vaneigem's short chapter on humiliation points to key elements of modern humiliation. Vaneigem views our current circumstances as continuous with those of the last 200 years, so modern variations exist but share in their essentials with the past. He sees us as atomized individuals jostling each other through our days in a mutual exchange of humiliation. Indoctrinated, "everywhere it's hat's off to family, marriage, sacrifice, work, inauthenticity."³⁶ We are subject to an "immense conditioning machine" of "city planning, publicity, ideology, culture."³⁷ The only way out of this, he argues, is 'the gift' (an alternative to economic integration), self-realization, and collectivity. We are dying of stress because of modern life and this gives rise to the urge towards a counter "violence" which is the beginning of tactics. (Not murder or terrorism but not humanism either—which also creates the conditions from which we suffer).

> Despite their mistakes and their poverty, I see in the historical experience of workers' councils (1917, 1921, 1934, 1956), and in the pathetic search for friendship and love, a single and inspiring reason not to despair over present 'reality'.³⁸

The loss of self-sufficiency along with our dependency on and integration into an economic system has many other effects, of course: stress and anxiety from the possibility of poverty and our potential humiliation from being unable to consume to specific levels; an increased need for servility to bosses and teachers for the same reasons; an increased corporate dominance over life and politics; sameness and the loss of manifestations of local culture; nature taken over and sold back to us as commodities; the destruction of the environment to manufacture commodities; the envisioning of all needs as commodities and human interactions in economic terms; the sickness resulting from over-consumption, etc. The servitude of labour, in order to consume enough to avoid humiliation, is itself a form of normative humiliation.

Surveillance and policing have reached astonishing new levels. Canada is now following the U.S. model of making the prison system the centre of the economy, of imprisoning the inessential or problematic for long periods (e.g. the 'native problem' where natives are vastly over-represented in prisons), and of directing tax dollars to the prison system.

Plutocracy, globalization and political dominance by economic power makes a final sham of the idea that we are part of democracies; that we can effect change society through the state and the vote. The lack of autonomy in every respect and the need to reform ourselves to accord with the demands of authority lead to both normative and psychological humiliation. The commodification of land and increasingly every sort of natural resource renders the possibility of communal self-sufficiency as more and more unlikely.

Avishai Margalit attempts to refute the idea that gaining autonomy and self-sufficiency would in itself be sufficient to overcome humiliation (as if levels of consumption is how human dignity is maintained). He wants to insist on liberal institutions so prioritizes what he terms 'decency,' arguing that life without acceptable levels of consumption is humiliating.

> A Tolstoyan commune may be a non humiliating society by virtue of the fact that it contains no ruling institutions, but it is not a decent society insofar as its living conditions of grinding poverty are perceived as humiliating.[39]

I'm not clear why he uses the adjective 'grinding' other than to colour his argument, but his supposition is that one can't live in a 'decent' society if you feel it to be humiliating. This is true enough, but he speaks as if living in a commune violates some universal law of affluence, invariably making people poor, and humiliating them. He is using poverty in its ideological sense, that the absence of certain objects and being out of the economic mainstream, is automatically demeaning. This is to articulate the suppositions of the West, of development, and to advocate for them. It is the terms of colonialism so fails to recognize that succumbing to these ideas is no different than succumbing to the other ways in which we are ruled. Colonialism and all forms of power always seek to define what we should feel humiliated by. Liberalism furthers humiliation as surely as conservative views do.

Consumerism abrogates the religious notion that we are being watched and should feel anxiety and potential humiliation because of it. Consuming is an ethical good. For example, dressing up is seditious at heart (like much play, like charivari), and is a way of thwarting socio-religious ideas that our identity is eternal, in the image of God, subject to control. In the world of consumption, dressing up loses the quality of radical playing with identity (e.g. the inversion of gender that is seen in the charivari). Identity becomes the target of consumerism, to make oneself over with purchases and discipline, to meet the gaze without humiliation, to 'express yourself' in a way that identifies you as a consumer of an identity as much as a consumer of a thing. (Academic attempts to create a semiotics of fashion, to speak of a language of clothing, to supposedly see through people, to ridicule them as pathetic, is a pretentious endeavour and conservative at heart, and also the basis of marketing. Something that says very little since it

Anti consumerism stencil
Photo by Edgar Fabiano, Wikimedia Commons

misses the radical and seditious elements of play. Such analysis reinforces the view of humans as only malleable and pathetic consumers.)

The expansion of law always leads to an expansion of crime (e.g. the charivari). Craig Grimes on a character about to turn to crime:

> Ida drove her twenty-year old unlicensed car through traffic. She'd only taken it today rather than face a two-hour bus ride in the early morning. She accelerated, waited at a light, gunned it, stopped, waited, waited, waited, until she was ready to scream. She would pass eight-hundred and fifty-seven signs on the way home directing her about what she

could or couldn't do. Around her, drivers ran red lights and took corners by cutting through parking lots, frustrated, near road-raging petty criminals. Even when control exists with the best of intentions it is human nature to resist it. Today Ida felt the frustration of driving as just more humiliation. Just more banal totalitarian power that strips one of self-governance, like the Taylorism at Plastican, like bully bosses, and even the billboards she passed of people on Caribbean beaches telling her what to dream. She resented the failure of her dreams and the carrot the ads dangled that kept her toiling at crap jobs. She felt an overwhelming anger at the million humiliations that came from simply living her drab, powerless existence.[40]

Since the city is not controlled by its residents, it can only contain lives of constant humiliation; humiliation compounded by traffic noise, pollution and the general prison conditions of life organized around consumption, production and social control.

Can liberalized planning return to us control over the urban community? To take back the streets which were stolen at the point that they became arteries of traffic, subject to engineered planning and the employment of pseudoscience on behalf of economic interests?

There are those who argue (e.g. Ivan Illich, John Zerzan) that we are increasingly part of systems, like traffic, where the very possibility of autonomy is eliminated.

A tool, argues Illich,[41] (in the case of traffic management, the automobile) shapes us rather than vice-versa. This is not through the pseudoscientific management of traffic or city planning only but of these in conjunction with police, ambulance, insurance, car sales, commerce and so on. All are now parts of a system working together. There is no effective alternative, you must integrate yourself into the system in order to travel through the city or to live in it. It is a mental construct as much as a physical one, controlling our imaginations and how we analyze a situation, and how we evaluate success.

The notion of 'shadow planning' (where so-called scientific laws are adapted to the demands of political power) undermines the pretension of planners and engineers to be working according to scientific laws. But the notion of system is useful to get at the fact that we have moved beyond politics, locking ourselves into a modernity that cannot be affected in any real way by changing colonial managers. The replacement of conservative politicians and planners with liberal ones wouldn't make any significant difference. Planners cannot help us here. A system is above politics. (Even Jane Jacob's followers try to replicate a diverse ecosystem; but it is still external planning, and all planning seeks control over social relations. We would still be part of a system which humiliates.)

But the word 'system' here is still a metaphor. (New engineers, in addition to being trained in their speciality are also trained in systems management.) It suggests that human behaviour can be controlled in the way a machine's behaviour can be. Although the ambition of system planners, at heart, is to manufacture stupidity, to eliminate creativity and every semblance of autonomous action, they fail. System managers criminalize challenges and they become morally reprehensible, but human will suggests that human robotization is not inevitable. Control generates more laws but also more lawbreaking (e.g. the system of traffic through a city frequently contains the illegal and ad hoc — running lights, u-turns etc. — and traffic movement may even require the illegal e.g. without illegal left turns traffic would stop). It is not to suggest that traffic rules are an imposition on our freedom worth railing about to note that the vast increase in laws that a system needs, to eliminate all variation and creativity, or to protect the economy and the production of junk (e.g. mandatory insurance, lights and horn, no talking on one's cell phone, increased sig-

Mulberry Street NYC, circa 1900
Traffic control would soon enforce the public road as the domain of the new auto technology used for the rapid 'circulation' (stealing the term from biology) of goods and workers — i.e. engineering creating pseudoscience from real science, arguing its case in the name of safety and a better life on behalf of industry, and defining the terms of the debate from then on.

nage and direction about speed, turns and other movement, etc.) all lead to an increase in illegality. Such is human nature. Such is the demand of autonomy when faced by a system. Even though people approve of safety measures, like stop signs, they become frustrated with the volume of rules made in the name of safety that a system requires.

A surfeit of laws to protect us renders independence highly unlikely (e.g. all the laws governing the building of structures means that we must rely on experts to build a house, to get approval to build, a mortgage, insurance etc.) making us helpless to act on our own; the home-building skills of our forebears gone.

Work is another example of the new centrality of systems. Modern work takes us well beyond Taylorism and the assembly line. Taylorism's real value—which has often been asserted—was not in its ability to save money on the assembly line but in its ability to control. More recent endeavours like 'process improvement' have extended this to all jobs within an organization, defining them as parts of a system, and analyzing them with systems models. Like Taylorism, these strip creativity, intelligence and variability—providing a better means of attaching a dollar value to all human motion, and to police behaviour—and treat humans as dumb machines capable of ignoring the mind-numbing boredom of the endless repetition of some task (where people's work tasks are reduced on the premise that they will work faster if they are performing the same task over

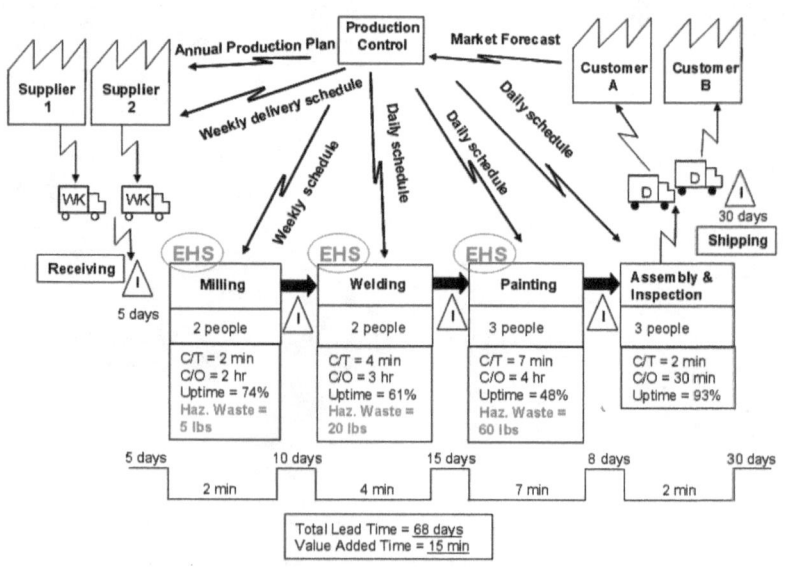

U.S. E.P.A. LEAN and Environment Toolkit,

and over). Businesses become top heavy with management layers whose role is surveillance and the perfection of the system.

Some of the psychological effects on workers, of the engineering of human labour, are an increased psychological alienation from having no process input (in addition to the normative alienation from not owning the means of production), intense boredom, and higher levels of work errors. But, of course, since human beings are involved, there is also an increase in 'illegal' activities like retaliatory destruction (not part of an articulated critique, but not mindlessness; action with a definite target). Like our drive through traffic, work is marked by frequent occasions of passive resistance, slacking off and causing errors. Humanity compels it.[42]

William Ian Miller relates the following anecdote:

> I teach a seminar for which the catalogue carries the name Legal Anthropology ... One year it was called "Legal Anthropology: Violence." The next year, obsessed with humiliation, I decided to make this chapter the core of the seminar, which got posted during preregistration simply as "Humiliation, Prof. Miller." In the violence seminar there were two men for every woman; in the humiliation seminar there were six women for every man...
>
> The gendering of humiliation as feminine is intimately connected to vulgar views of the sex act. In this view, men poke, prod, pierce, penetrate; their actions rely heavily on verbs that cause deflation. And what is being deflated if not the pretension of women to moral equivalence with men? Women are on the bottom, on the humus; they are brought low, done dirt, subjected to host of metaphors which capture the root sense of humiliate. In this view of sex, a view held by some feminists [radical feminist Catharine A. MacKinnon is cited], the sexual act can only humiliate women in the eyes of men and often in their own eyes as well.[43]

The "gendering of humiliation" is not because the "feminine is intimately connected to vulgar views of the sex act." They are only being conjoined here, by a marginal group, one that has no impact on what most women feel. Women's ambitions are often deflated but this does not depend on a 'vulgar view of the sex act' to be the case. Normative and psychological humiliation, and shame in women's lives existed and was discussed long before radical feminism. Feminine humiliation, with its own unique qualities, is a vast subject that involves the normative conditions of masculine authority, the lack of gender equality, the suppression of the female voice, and the psychological imposition of shame and humiliation for dress, speech, uncontrolled sexuality and any other action that threatens male authority.

The Mocking Serenade

The radical feminist view of women and humiliation, as outlined by Miller, is just another case of ascribing humiliation in order to control women, to hijack the notion, so does not get to the real sources of humiliation. It is an extremely anti-sexual and conservative view that tries to rule over women's sex lives, trying to convince that consensual heterosexual sex is always an occasion of humiliation, of injury and abasement. The 'feminist' proponents of this view are just more people seeking to manipulate the personal lives of women through ascribing humiliation and shame. They use fanciful assertions about what men think and feel, and the "vulgar views of the sex act" (e.g. since nothing is punctured, nothing is deflated), and ignore the men who contradict these views by putting women on pedestals, romanticizing sex, etc.

Women "on the humus" presumably comes from the view of sex as dirty which stems from the focus on cleanliness which originated in Hebrew law and was applied to men as much as women.[44] Individual acts, it was decided, could affect and pollute the entire tribe so needed to be regulated. There were to be rituals around menstruation, but male circumcision was also proscribed, and male on male sex now carried with it a death sentence because semen supposedly polluted the body (and thus the body politic) in a way that didn't happen with married heterosexual sex (since the aim was to be fruitful and multiply). Radical feminism reinforces the idea of sex as dirty, now ascribing this characteristic to all male-female sex. The use of shame is, as it always was, a means for the powerful, or those attempting to gain authority and influence, to control people.

Segment of an image taken at a Slut Walk,
photo by Hugh Lee, June 4, 2011, Flickr

Santiago, August 4, 2011, student cacerolazo, photo by Simenon, Flickr

Casserole, Rosemont, Montréal (Québec),
photos by Francis Bourgouin. Flickr

5. Modern Charivari

In Québec, in 2012, students staged protests when the government promised to raise university tuition rates, but what prompted huge charivaris across the province (and the country) was the attempt by the government to legally prohibit such protests "after peaceful protests were met with police violence in Montréal and Victoriaville."[45]

On May 22, 2012, in response to the passage of Bill 78 and in commemoration of 100 days since the beginning of the student strike, another march took place, with tens of thousands of marchers and approximately 1,000 arrests. Organizers spun this event as "The single biggest act of civil disobedience in Canadian history." By May 24, 2012, the "Casseroles" series of nightly protests had rapidly expanded to most Montréal residential neighborhoods outside of the usual protest routes. Inspired by the cacerolazos of Chile in 1971, these involved residents banging on pots and pans from their windows or taking to the streets with their kitchenware at 8 o'clock.[46]

Control over the street itself was central, as it always is in charivari.

Since the point of the [Québec]protests is to audibly flout Law 78, the fact that they can be heard much further than they can be seen helps make this lawbreaking an expressly public and political act. Montréal mayor Gerard Tremblay acknowledged as much: "They can stay on their balconies to make noise. I'm in Outremont (a wealthy enclave next to Mile End and the Plateau, another epicenter of the protests) and I can hear it. No need to go onto the street, to walk around and paralyse Montréal." The volume's territorial reach also works as an invitation to join in, either by banging along on one of Montréal's ubiquitous porches, or by entering the procession itself.[47]

The Montréal charivaris brought together many in the community to exercise their power against the government, not only for increasing tuition rates but for attempting to extend its authority and control.
This was taken much further in Argentina.
In 2001, in Argentina, bank accounts were frozen to deal with economic collapse. Immediately, without coordination, people from all walks of life, of all ages, took to the streets banging pots and pans. Five consecutive governments were forced out over the next weeks. People sang, 'Que se vayan todos' ('They all must go').

The Mocking Serenade

Crisis del 20 de diciembre de 2001 en Argentina,
photo by PRFOTOBAIRES from Arte y Fotografía

Marina Sitrin writes that as "a product of being in the streets together," people began to organize in workplaces and "unemployed neighbourhoods."

> Land and workplaces were recuperated, a barter network of millions of people developed, and the movements linked with one another.[48]

She argues that the charivari created a rupture with the past, generated a new self-confidence and bravery, and empowered people to change without leaders.

> This was not just a break with parties from formal institutions of power, but also with radical and revolutionary left parties, from the Peronists to the Trotskyist.[49]

Sitrin argues that it is the following characteristics that sustain this "revolution of the everyday." (Not only the title echos Vaneigem but the sort of changes begun by charivari are those which he indicated were central to the reversal of humiliation).

- horizontalidad — a form of direct decision making that rejects hierarchy and works as an ongoing process

- autogestión—a form of self-management with an implied form of horizontalidad[50]

- concrete projects related to sustenance and survival

- territory—the use and recuperation of physical and metaphorical space

- changing social relationships—including changing identity with regard to the personal and collective

- politica afectiva—a politics and social relationship based on love and trust

- self-reflection—individual and collective, as to the radical changes taking place and how they break from past ways of organizing

- autonomy, challenging 'power over' and creating 'power with' —sometimes using the state, but at the same time, against and beyond the state[51]

In Sitrin's view, the Argentinian experiments are significant in challenging notions about revolution, leadership, value, power and the role of love and friendship in radical change. Ethical responsibility becomes central to any form of radical change or old forms of exploitation and hierarchy are reintroduced.

6. The Spirit of Charivari

In its essence the purpose of satire—whether verse or prose—is aggression. (When whimsical, sentimental, or "poetic" it is a sort of bastard humour.) Satire has a great big glaring target. If successful, it blasts a great big hole in the center. Directness there must be and singleness of aim: it is all aim, all trajectory.

—Wyndham Lewis

Angelique Haugerud on satirical activism:

In these ironic humorists we can detect echoes of late-medieval and Renaissance carnival, rituals of status reversal, charivaris, "festivals of resistance," as well as more recent Dadaists, Brechtian tactics, Situationists, surrealists, Yuppie guerilla theater, Bread and Puppet Theatre, Guerilla Girls, Ladies Against Women, Code Pink, and Reclaim the Streets.[52]

Haugerud is speaking here of *Bush For Billionaires* and other manifestations of this street theatre group that began in 2004. Dressed as billionaires, in the attire of conspicuous consumption, like ball gowns and tuxedos, they go by names such as: *Phil T Rich, Iona Bigga Yacht*, and *Noah Countability*. And they carry professionally printed placards with slogans like: *Corporations Are People Too, Taxes Are Not For Everyone, It's a Class War And We're Winning*, and *Thank You For Paying Our Fair Share*. The concerns they raise include: the dominance of wealth in politics, income disparity, unfair taxation, corporate welfare, and the myth of market self-regulation.

The Bush for Billionaire's irony is interesting and smart. Like charivari they use reverse humiliation, costuming, and humour, but unlike charivari they remain within the law, protesting and not practising self-management. This is true of a number of other satiric activists who use pranks (like culture jammers who issue brilliant false press releases to force companies to counter them with explicit statements about their behaviour—'no we do not accept responsibility for our actions,' etc.)[53] Sometimes individuals, like graffiti artists, break the law, but their anonymity and radicality can be quickly absorbed into the art market as purchasable dissent.

Lumping satiric street theatre with charivari or Situationist actions (revolution) is inaccurate, as they are of different natures and effect. As part of this levelling, charivari is generally used as a synonym for carnival, although they are very different. Carnival was a calendar day of celebration and excess that allowed for inversion (carnival/lent). But carnival can be seen as a sort of safety valve. The church co-opted carnival. While carnival was evidence of subversive feeling, carnival and lent both reinforced the same thing in the end, the power of the church. But charivari was not something that could be co-opted. The church only ever condemned charivaris for their lawlessness. Even when charivaris were concerned with marriage they were always a challenge to the power of the church and the state.

> There are scores of festivals, fairs, and ritual occasions that share many of the essential features of carnival itself. The Feast of Fools, charivari, coronations, periodic market fairs, harvest celebrations, spring fertility rights [sic], and even traditional elections share something of the carnivalesque... What all these occasions seem to share is that they are socially defined in some important ways as being out of the ordinary. Normal rules of social intercourse are not enforced, and either the wearing of actual disguises or the anonymity conferred by being part of a large crowd amplifies a general air of license — licentiousness. Much of the writing on carnival emphasizes the spirit of physical abandon, its celebration of the body through dancing, gluttony, open sexuality, and general immodesty. The classical carnival figure is a fat, lusty eater and drinker... What is most interesting about carnival is the way it allows certain things to be said, social forms of social power to be exercised that are muted or repressed outside this ritual sphere. The anonymity of the setting, for example, allows the social sanctions of the small community normally exercised through gossip to assume a more full-throated voice... carnival is 'the people's informal courtroom'... Disapproval that would be dangerous or socially costly to vent at other times is sanctioned during carnival.[54]

Modern carnival always reflects dual aspects. There are elements of subversion at the same time as there is a venting that strengthens authority. It is a time set apart, with night-time morality that challenges the day-to-day moral codes. Modern sports are examples of this (compare the image below with a photo of rugby or American football). Although charivari is also based on play, it is an attempt to impose its own rules in an antisocial way. Soccer hooliganism has aspects of charivari because it is a playing out of folk football which attacked enclosure (fences were knocked down as participants moved between the competing towns), so it was a defence of subsistence farming communities. Soccer hooliganism is, at its heart, still an actual and not symbolic attack on authority.[55]

Occupy Wall Street has appropriately been analyzed as carnival. (It also has aspects of charivari such as the banging of pots and pans, and the focus on re-claiming land.) In this case, the simultaneous presence of competing aspects

The Spirit of Charivari

Battle Between Carnival and Lent by Jan Miense Molenaer, 1633-4,

that both challenge and reinforce authority should be recognized. It is a different sort of phenomena than the anarchist actions in places like Argentina.

Claire Tancons on OWS:

> Just as the economy is the crux of the movement's concerns, it is also at the core of Carnival… Carnival was widely practiced in the Americas, where colonization and slavery replaced European feudalism and servitude, and where plantations afforded experiments with capitalism that would later develop into British industrialism. In the Old World as in the New, Carnival thrived off the extreme disparity between masters, their subjects, or slaves — what today we would call wealth inequality. Role reversals alleviated a brutally divisive social system by crowning servants and slaves king for a day. Carnival created an opportunity for society to cohere anew, at least for the duration of the festivities. With this understanding of the structural dynamic of Carnival, it is not surprising to see carnivalesque strands appearing in America's frayed social fabric at a time when the rich have never been richer and the poor never poorer. Just as for [David] Graeber the current debt crisis is part of a larger story, so is OWS's carnival. As Graeber explains,

"Throughout history, debt has served as a way for states to control their subjects and extract resources from them (usually to finance wars). And when enough people got in enough debt, there was usually some kind of revolt."[Drake Bennett, "David Graeber: The Anti-Leader of Occupy Wall Street," *Bloomberg Business Week*, October 26, 2011.]...
In stalwart carnival countries, the century-old festival has failed in recent decades to generate political momentum around key societal issues. Instead, it has succumbed to forms of rampant consumerism and escapist fun that are as remote from political relevance as any other mainstream entertainment.[56]

Graeber notes the propensity for societies to revolt because of debt. The qualification I would make here about tying this comment to carnival is that carnival is not revolt, but charivari is. Debt can be an impetus for charivari.

In pointing, above, to the lumping and levelling of satire with other forms of radical action that is sometimes made — which obscures their distinctive qualities — I don't mean to suggest that some forms are insignificant. Satirists, protestors and pieing, for example, draw attention to important issues and can have a substantial effect on the fortunes of politicians and corporations. They can be like carnival though, having only a short-term impact, for a news cycle, and then fall from view (meanwhile New Orleans has not been rebuilt or the people repatriated, oil still pours into the Gulf of Mexico, and South American miners are still being poisoned, etc.). Some forms of dissent are more in line with certain formal aspects of charivari although they can arise from the same impulses as the carnivalesque. In recent English riots the looting seems to have been directly aimed at international stores rather than those owned by neighbours. These actions actually place the participants at greater risk than they would face in a typical charivari. (The Black Bloc does not seem to have much effect with their property destruction, other than to garner media attention, but it is improperly branded as 'violence,' as was the case with the Luddites and others, and this allows protesters to be met with physical violence by authority.)

The charivari is, at heart, a form of street theatre. There are a number of examples of modern street theatre that invert humiliation.

Happenings developed in the 1950's as artists and musicians (John Cage staged the first happening) sought to break down the barrier between audience and performer, to challenge the class nature and exclusivity of art.

According to Bradford D. Martin, there was also a response from the art world to [the official charivari of] McCarthyism and the attempt to maintain a separation between politics and art. Because of it, a number of forms of street

The Spirit of Charivari

A Public Hanging, Happening 2005 at Atlas Meats, Meatpacking District, Manhattan, New York City, NY (U.S.),

theatre developed, drawing from various sources, happenings among them, which attempted to make street theatre that was explicitly political [this unity was also central to the Situationists]. All had elements of charivari.

> After performances of *Paradise Now* (1968-1970), the Living Theatre accompanied its audience into the streets to begin what it called the "beautiful nonviolent anarchist revolution." The Diggers performed puppet shows on the streets of San Francisco's Haight-Ashbury neighborhood and distributed free food in Golden Gate Park... GAAG's [Guerrilla Art Action Group] guerrilla actions subverted museums' institutional prestige by disturbing business-as-usual, provoking authorities and challenging the art world by exposing its relationship to the American military-industrial complex.[57]

The Diggers of Haight-Ashbury of the late sixties, in particular, were very much in line with the charivari in inverting the conditions of everyday life with satire, and in combining theatre with forms of self management and communal living. They emphasized personal freedom, sexual freedom, ethical responsibility, and a refusal to recognize the money economy by giving food and other items in 'free stores,' offering free medical help, free places to sleep, free concerts. (These activities were not related to poverty and were not charity or approved morality, but a way of living outside of the money economy. Things were free even to those with money.)

> The modern Diggers undertook numerous initiatives to subvert the prevailing capitalist economy, actively committing themselves to implementing practical means for people in their community to live without money and publicizing their work with events such as the "Death of Money" parade.[58]

> "Refuse to consume." This advice equated freedom with "failure," or refusal, to participate in the consumer economy. "Everything we do is free because we are failures"... to Show Love is to fail.[59]

Martin notes that the group wished to avoid recuperation through the use of anonymity, and sought to achieve integration with others in the community—but avoiding the tyranny of community by emphasizing personal freedom. They attacked hippies (as media creation) as part of a general attack on consumerism, and had little interest in participating in spectacle (as the Yippies did) but, having a more complex relationship with the issue, did, on occasion, try to manipulate the media to help them speak to the public. Street theatre did this as well, and was at the heart of their activities. In one instance they drove a flatbed truck containing a moving festival through the financial district urging the workers to leave work and join them.

Since the aim of the Diggers was not charity, they did not evolve into this. They turned over the soup kitchen and free medical clinic to others. They integrated with people from other groups and encamped to communes in the country where many still live today.

The Diggers (who dropped the name and took on various other monikers), reflects a particular type of activism. The emphasis on love should not be misunderstood as a cliche hippie idealism, but was a recognition that love demands radical politics with ethical responsibility at the heart of it. Love, in this sense, is not that reserved for mankind, for the generalized love of a species, for sympathy and charity, but the ethical basis of new forms of social relationships based on mutual responsibility and equality at the centre of social change.[60]

The Diggers experience also highlighted the inevitability of legal conflicts when attempting to live change. Theirs wasn't (like 'civil disobedience') meant to provoke the law, to initiate a challenge, but the inevitable outcome of living without regard to authority. (Squatters are another instance of trying to fly under the legal radar.) When law is meant to protect private ownership and thievery by the powerful (obscured by the fuss made over petty infractions) then the illegal is demanded. Diggers engaged in theft, did not obtain legal permits for gatherings, and ignored legal codes for crash pads. (A good

The Spirit of Charivari

Gargantua, a lithography by Honoré Daumier
Daumier's 1832 satiric caricature of King Louis-Phillipe as a useless blob
stealing from the people and expelling financial feces to benefit the parasites
of the court, got him 6 months in jail.

deal of their concern was to help people during the onrush of hippies into San Francisco during the sixties).

Of course, law is a means to quell dissent (and the charivari is an attempt to control the law). The city, embarrassed by the Diggers for drawing attention to the city's inability to help the hungry, passed regulations to hinder companies giving the Diggers free food to dispense!

What the Diggers were doing (following their own standards of justice) was different (for the most part, because its actions did not respect the law) from groups that use illegal acts like defacement and public nudity to get media attention, with the inevitable arrests becoming part of the spectacle. Generally speaking, the charivari is different from street theatre like Femen (an organized group of women who protest naked or semi-naked with slogans painted on their chests, generally arrested in public spectacles) where the events are only media events and there are ten men with cameras for every protester.

Which is not to say that public nudity may not be a statement about the treatment and ownership of bodies. Muslim women posting photos on their

The Mocking Serenade

Sin Memoria Me Moria, Corporación Colombiana de teatro, by Guache, Wikimedia Commons
The Columbian Theatre Corporation is an activist grassroots group. 'False positives' refers to the people murdered by the Columbian military who were then designated as guerillas in headcount statistics. This is a further example of how, when success becomes measurable simply in quanitative terms, morality and other considerations disappear. The Colombian military is no different than most corporations. The protester is presumably a bloodied corpse to enact what happened, but also to garner media attention.

websites, their exposed chests bearing the message, 'Fuck your morals,' makes the connection between morality and power, and posting the pictures is an act of independence and a statement about who owns their body. Of course some will complain that this reinforces masculine objectification of women as sex objects—which always has a very puritanical, anti-nakedness feel—but the acts seem to be about celebrating human sexual freedom and are not done for the benefit of voyeurs.

Taking control of various parts of the city has been central to Reclaim the Streets, to the creation of Temporary Autonomous Zones (Hakim Bey) like OWS, etc. Control of an area theoretically reclaims the commons in some sense. It may not occasion subsistence farming or other inversions of colonialism, but it allows for the creation of different social relations and a temporary respite from the takeover of roads for commerce. Control of land is central to colonial takeovers and the maintenance of capitalism, so it is not coincidental that OWS was quashed in its physical manifestation using laws that guard land ownership. (But activities like those staged by Reclaim the Street seem to have devolved into street parties held in agreement with authorities who plan around the disruption. It is that dual aspect of carnival at work. The ritual of dissent.)

The ability to have and control land is critical to any kind of autonomous alternatives to economic integration. Colonialism always steals land and renders this unlikely.

Rory Carroll writing about Oakland, California and the debt crisis:

> From 2007 the foreclosure crisis hit like a "Greek tragedy", according to a 2012 report from the Urban Strategies Council, a local thinktank. "What began with an over-inflated housing bubble and the targeting of predatory loan products to homeowners of colour has ultimately peaked with the displacement of thousands." Some 10,508 homes were foreclosed between 2007 and 2012, with poor, black families bearing the brunt. This created a "colossal opportunity" for wealthy individuals and corporations to snap up real estate, said the report... Oakland's activists also despair over the city's plan to integrate hundreds of cameras, sensors and data feeds in a new Domain Awareness Center, calling it a tool of mass surveillance masked as an anti-crime measure. Adding insult to injury, the police department, which was fined $1m for brutalising Occupy protesters, hosts an annual event, called Urban Shield, which showcases tactics and technology for crowd control to other police forces.[61]

Crisis is always a pretext to disenfranchise people of their land and to destroy communities.

> When the hurricane hit, New Orleans' political and business leaders, White and Black, saw it as an opportunity to purge the city of its most conspicuous concentrations of Black poverty, with the added benefit that they could redevelop these cleansed zones into highly profitable housing and tourist attractions...tens of thousands of New Orleanians, most of them poor, have joined a permanent and involuntary Katrina diaspora. In the five years since the hurricane, the city's population has shrunk by roughly 100,000, from its height of 455,000 one month before Katrina.
>
> Columbia Parc was conceived in the days after the storm, as a group of New Orleans business leaders and foundation executives gathered to take advantage of the opportunity inherent in the displacement of virtually the entire Black working class population of the city. They incorporated as the Bayou District Foundation, a private nonprofit

redevelopment authority with a board of directors that included some of the region's top real estate, tourism, and banking leaders, and patched together a plan to socially, economically, and geographically remake a large swath of the city's 7th Ward.

The federal Department of Housing and Urban Development (HUD) cooperated readily with the Bayou District Foundation and other developers interested in privatizing public housing. [62]

As a result: poor neighbourhoods were demolished; kinship networks destroyed; aims to 'develop' and socially re-engineer African American communities had disastrous results (housing was only one aspect of this, e.g. many schools were privatized, firing local teachers, and no longer allowing unions etc.); aid money went not to poor renters but to landlords; poor areas were replaced with profit centres of mixed housing with only small numbers of public housing units; in some new developments public housing units were available only to those with jobs, with no criminal record etc.; there were less new housing units than those destroyed and the rents were much higher (amid a general attempt to gentrify the city) so homelessness increased (and the homeless were harassed to move on); some people lost homes because they could not prove title to their property because it had been passed down since the end of slavery. Public money has, however, been made available for military growth in the area and for the expansion of prison spaces (filled disproportionately with young black men).[63]

While actions in cities, like community gardens or squatting, are still possible, the more likely terrain to create autonomous realms may be the countryside. But, remembering the warnings of people like Paul Virilio, this may already be a closed issue. The city is a done deal where we are all refugees with no connection to land, detached from it, unable to escape either upwards in condos or outwards in suburbs. It is the same in the countryside according to Virillio:

> It is well and truly underway, this sort of post-urban revolution that will drive the twenty-first century. It's a portable revolution, a révolution de l'emport, with consequences for the history of planning and development that could prove singularly more devastating than last century's revolution in industrial transport. This is why, right now, the rug is being pulled out from under sedentary settlement of an urban species which is, in the end, as threatened as the rural species was up until the revelation of food insecurity that has now hit us, with the totally symptomatic business of cereal based biofuels.[64]

Virilio and others also remain deeply pessimistic about the promise of technology to free us. Technology is always tied to oppression and the impossibility of autonomy. Among those who will insist on the use of technology however, there are some who attempt to use it in ways that increase some degree of autonomy (which always needs to be qualified, since all technology creates junk, destroys the environment, and initially strengthens the capitalist economy). Still, it is notable as a site of modern charivari.

Cyberspace is likened to the effort to reclaim land, and often envisioned as if it were physical space where some people fight to maintain it as a commons against the attempts by the state, the military and the market to control it,[65] a collusion evident in the widely publicized stories of NSA surveillance, for example.

The oft quoted "A Declaration of the Independence of Cyberspace," by the Electronic Frontier Foundation puts it:

> You do not know our culture, our ethics, or the unwritten codes that already provide our society more order than can be obtained by any of your impositions.

Durand and Vergne on cyber piracy:

> Once again, the alliance between a sovereign state and monopolistic organizations nurtures a milieu that delineates the norms applicable to a partially uncharted territory. And once again, this situation gives rise to organized piracy by excluding groups of people and pushing them to the fringes. These pirate organizations stand up against the state and its accompanying legitimate corporations. We may even wonder whether AT&T, Microsoft and Google are to American sovereignty what the VOC was to the sovereignty of the United Provinces [i.e. The Netherlands, at the time when sea piracy began] — that is, instruments of normalized capitalist deterritorialization disguised as corporations.[66]

Another area of contestation involves computer code, which is described as language, and the patents that govern it as comparable to trying to patent language. Hacktivism is a vast subject in itself. It supports the idea of a commons through the development of open source and free software, that is creative and fun, is not a product of a hierarchical group, is frequently illegal, and uses humiliation as a means of resistance.

> For many, being a hacker is about autonomy, politics and fun but above all it is about making a difference in the world that presents itself to them; whether that is breaking illicitly into computers or writing the software someone wants.[67]

The Mocking Serenade

The use of humiliation can be seen in the efforts to refuse market and state dominance over cyberspace and technology. Wikileaks famously leaks classified and secret documents that expose the workings of states and militaries. And individuals do something similar, on a much smaller scale, when they film the actions of police and then post the videos online. I think here, as one example, of the 'Officer Bubbles' video that was passed around by email and even posted by an alternative news organization on Youtube (and viewed a million times). It shows a policeman harassing a woman for blowing bubbles during the G20 Summit in Toronto. It was a clear demonstration of the out of control power of police who'd been given free reign so set about terrorizing the citizenry. Posting a video of Officer Bubbles was a response to the power play by police and the violence of officers (who arrested the bubble blower and over a thousand people who were simply on the streets at the time) not with reciprocal violence but by humiliating him. Posting videos of this sort is increasingly common. (I accept E.P. Thompson's comment that shaming is most effective when both parties are part of the same small community. Bubbles may have been completely unaffected by the humiliation.)

In Closing

There is no definitive form of charivari, even ancient charivaris varied widely, so looking at modern instances of charivari-like activity is only to say that they share such and such a characteristic with their predecessors. They are also very different. But, in the examples above, what is essentially carried over is that charivari is not a political protest over a specific policy, even if limited in its scope, but is a fundamental challenge to the cornerstones of modern society, dominated by joint monopolies of power — political, military, and economic — resisting the movement to global uniformity and displacement of people which now renders them unable to live outside of the new systems. All these monopolistic forms of authority are colonialist in their use of blunt force, surveillance, brainwashing institutions, laws and humiliation.

While charivari inverts humiliation I don't wish to imply that it is the only form of radical response worthy of note. Every small act, creating a neighbourhood vegetable garden, a free daycare or co-op, paying under the table, lying, sabotage, and a million other initiatives and necessary illegalities reinforce the same ambitions to live outside of market dominance and to increase autonomy. Morality is central, but not the heteronomous morality of authority, which as often as not demands its contravention.

Russell Brand:

> The only reason to vote is if the vote represents power or change. I don't think it does. I fervently believe that we deserve more from our democratic system than the few derisory tit-bits tossed from the carousel of the mighty, when they hop a few inches left or right. The lazily duplicitous servants of The City expect us to gratefully participate in what amounts to little more than a political hokey cokey where every four years we get to choose what colour tie the liar who leads us wears.[68]

There has only ever been one reason for charivari. Charivari is the option of not appealing for change but of simply acting autonomously.

.

Charivari, Montréal (Québec), June 2, 2012,
photo by Benoit Rochon. Wikimedia Commons
The wall graffiti reads: "Youth wakes up"
The banner reads: "Mothers are angry and united"

People began to display different coloured squares to express particular viewpoints. There is a black square on the banner: "The black square: Symbol of the anarchist groups implicated in the conflict. Those with this square believe that the system is intrinsically flawed and needs to change. They have also been commonly associated with the more extreme views on the conflict – and the more extreme beliefs in terms of actions. 'Anti-capitalism' has been another common term when discussing this symbol."[69]

End Notes

1. "From Sturton by Stow," James M. Carpenter collection in Cecil Sharp House.
2. Lynn Stephens, "Women Play Key Role in Oaxaca Struggle," North American Congress on Latin America 2006, 10 Sept. 2013 <http://nacla.org/news/women-play-key-role-oaxaca-struggle>
3. "2009 Icelandic financial crisis protests," Wikipedia, 10 Sept. 2013 <http://en.wikipedia.org/wiki/2009_Icelandic_financial_crisis_protests>
4. E.P. Thompson, "Rough Music Reconsidered," *Folklore* Vol. 103, No. 1, 1992, 3, 10 Sept. 2013 <http://www.csulb.edu/~ssayeghc/theory/wintertheory/rough%20music.pdf>
5. Naomi Klein, "All Of Them Must Go," 5 Feb.2009, 12 Sept. 2013 <http://www.naomiklein.org/articles/2009/02/all-them-must-go>
6. Thomas Hardy, *The Mayor of Casterbridge*. 10 Sept. 2013 <http://www.classicreader.com/book/66/39/>
7. Thompson.
8. Thompson 3.
9. Roslyn M. Frank, "Singing Duels and Social Solidarity: The Case of the Basque Charivari," acadamia.edu 2011, 12 Sept. 2013 <http://www.academia.edu/463572/Singing_Duels_and_Social_Solidarity_The_Case_of_the_Basque_Charivari>
10. *Frank* 3.
11. *Frank* 20.
12. *Frank* 1.
13. Dylan Thomas, *Rebecca's Daughter's* (Toronto: New Directions, 1982) 76.
14. Phil Carradice, "The Rebecca Riots." BBC 8 Nov. 2010, 10 Sept. 2013 <http://www.bbc.co.uk/blogs/wales/posts/the_rebecca_riot>
15. Thompson 17.
16. Norman Simms, "Ned Ludd's Mummers Play," *Folklore* Vol. 89, No 2, 1978, 170.
17. Evelin G. Lindner, "Dynamics of Humiliation in a Globalizing World," *International Journal of World Peace* Vol. XXIV No. 3, Sept. 2007, 21-22.
18. Avishai Margalit, *The Decent Society*, trans. Naomi Goldblum, (Cambridge: Harvard University Press, 1998).
19. Howard Zinn, *A People's History of American Empire* (New York: Metropolitan Books, 1988) 95.
20. Christopher Ryan and Cacilda Jethá, *Sex at Dawn: The Prehistoric origins of Modern Sexuality* (New York: Harper, 2010) 129.
21. Ryan and Jethá 171.
22. Antony Beevor, "An Ugly Carnival." *The Guardian*, 5 June 2009, 10 Sept. 2013 <http://www.theguardian.com/lifeandstyle/2009/jun/05/women-victims-d-

day-landings-second-world-war>
23. See for example, Vikram Dodd and Clare Dyer. "Guantánamo torture and humiliation still going on, says shackled Brito," *The Guardian*, 11 Dec. 2004, 10 Sept. 2013 <http://www.theguardian.com/world/2004/dec/11/politics.guantanamo>
24. Donal McGraith, *The Wild and the Free: Shane, Rousseau, Hippies* (Toronto: Charivari Press, 2014)
25. Pauline Greenhill, *Make the Night Hideous: Four English-Canadian Charivaris, 1881-1940* (Toronto: University of Toronto Press, 2010)
26. Greenhill 25.
27. Cecilia Dansyk, quoted in Greenhill, 21.
28. Dominique Moïsi, *The Geopolitics of Emotion: How Cultures of Fear, Humiliation, and Hope are Reshaping the World* (New York: Anchor Books, 2010) 56-57.
29. William Ian Miller, *Humiliation* (Ithaca: Cornell University Press, 1993) 138.
30. Jean-Jacques Rousseau, *The Social Contract and Discourses*, 1761, The Online Library of Liberty, 10 Sept. 2013 <http://oll.libertyfund.org/index.php?option=com_staticxt&staticfile=show.php%3Ftitle=638&layout=html>
31. Raoul Vaneigem, *The Revolution of Everyday Life*, trans. Donald Nicholson-Smith (Seattle: Left Bank Books, 1983). 14-23.
32. Seumas Milne, "The tide is turning against the scam that is privatisation," *The Guardian*, 9 July 2014, 9 July 2014 <http://www.theguardian.com/commentisfree/2014/jul/09/tide-turning-against-privatisation?CMP=EMCNEWEML6619I2>
33. Gerald Vizenor, Fugitive Poses, quoted in Thomas King, *The Inconvenient Indian: A Curious Account of Native People in North America* (Toronto: Doubleday Canada, 2012) 21.
34. Vaneigem 16.
35. Jean Baudrillard, *Simulacra and Simulation*, trans. Sheila Faria Glaser (Ann Arbor: University of Michigan Press, 1994) 8-9.
36. Vaneigem 18.
37. Vaneigem 21.
38. Vaneigem 18.
39. Margalit 20.
40. Craig Grimes, *The Aching Lust for Crime* (Toronto: Charivari Press, 2013) 19.
41. David Cayley and Ivan Illich, *The Rivers North of the Future: The Testament of Ivan Illich* (Toronto: House of Anansi Press, 2005) 201-205.
42. See James C. Scott, *Two Cheers for Anarchism* (Princeton: Princeton University Press, 2012) 7-22.
43. Miller 168-9.
44. See Eric Berkowitz, *Sex and Punishment: Four Thousand Years of Judging Desire* (Berkeley: Counterpoint, 2012).
45. "Cacerolazo," Wikipedia, 10 Sept. 2013 <http://en.wikipedia.org/wiki/

Cacerolazo>
46. "2012 Quebec student protests," Wikipedia, 10 Mar. 2014 <http://en.wikipedia.org/wiki/2012_Quebec_student_protests>
47. For a discussion of the relationship between rough music and the political role of the charivari (with particular reference to the Montréal protests) see Jonathan Sterne, "Quebec's casseroles: on participation, percussion and protest," *Sounding Out*, 4 June 2012, 10 Sept. 2013 <http://soundstudiesblog.com/2012/06/04/casseroles>
48. Marina A. Sitrin, *Everyday Revolutions: Horizontalism and Autonomy in Argentina* (New York: Zed Books, 2012) xiii.
49. Sitrin 56.
50. This is also an early Situationist position, e.g. the Autonomia in Italy, the Zapatista in Chiapas, etc.
51. Sitrin 3-4.
52. Angelique Haugerud, *No Billionaire Left Behind: Satirical Activism in America* (Stanford: Stanford University Press, 2013) 8.
53. See, for example, the satiric work of The Yes Men <http://theyesmen.org/>
54. James C. Scott, *Domination and the Arts of Resistance: Hidden Transcripts* (New Haven: Yale University Press, 2008) 173.
55. For a discussion of the above see Rod Dubey, I*ndecent Acts in a Public Place: Sports, Insolence and Sedition* (Toronto, Charivari Press, 1991)
56. Claire Tancons, "Occupy Wall Street: Carnival Against Capital? Carnivalesque as Protest Sensibility,"*e-flux JOURNAL* #30, Dec. 2011, 10 Sept. 2013 < http://www.e-flux.com/journal/occupy-wall-street-carnival-against-capital-carnivalesque-as-protest-sensibility>
57. Bradford D. Martin, *The Theater Is in the Street* (Amherst: University of Massachusetts Press, 2004) 6-7.
58. Martin 87.
59. Martin 97.
60. See Rod Dubey, …*beautiful in my worn clothes…The Transgressions of Love* (Toronto: Charivari Press, 2013).
61. Rory Carroll, "Oakland: the city that told Google to get lost." *The Guardian*, 11 Feb, 2014, 11 Feb. 2014 <http://www.theguardian.com/technology/2014/feb/10/city-google-go-away-oakland-california?CMP=EMCNEWEML6619I2>
62. Darwin BondGraham, "The Long Hurricane: The New Orleans Catastrophe Predates Katrina," *The Public Eye Magazine*, Vol. 25, No. 3, Fall 2010, 11 Feb. 2014 <http://www.publiceye.org/magazine/v25n3/the-long-hurricane.html>
63. For a summary of some changes see also Rachel E. Luft with Shana Griffin, "A Status Report on Housing in New Orleans after Katrina: An Intersectional Analysis," Katrina and the Women of New Orleans, Newcomb College Center for Research on Women, Dec. 2008, 11 Feb. 2014 <https://tulane.edu/nc-

crow/upload/NCCROWreport08-chapter5.pdf>
64. Paul Virillio, *The Futurism of the Instant: Stop-Eject* (Cambridge: Polity Press, 2010) 11.
65. See Rodolphe Durand and Jean-Philippe Vergne, *The Pirate Organization: Lessons From the Fringes of Capitalism* (Boston: Harvard Business Review Press, 2013).
66. Durand and Vergne 96-97.
67. Tim Jordan, *Hacking* (Cambridge: Polity Press, 2008) 4.
68. Russell Brand, "We deserve more from our democratic system." *The Guardian*, 5 Nov. 2013, 5 Nov. 2013 <http://www.theguardian.com/commentisfree/2013/nov/05/russell-brand-democratic-system-newsnight>
69. "Symbols of Quebec's Tumultuous Spring/Summer," Sylvestre Marketing, 27 Aug. 27, 2012 <http://sylvestremarketing.com/blog/symbols-of-quebecs-tumultuous-springsummer/>

Images

Cover: Top two images by Francois Bourgouin. Creative Commons <http://tinyurl.com/qesr2lg> and <http://tinyurl.com/q9qg3mx>
Bottom image by Boucheci. Creative Commons <http://tinyurl.com/nxcdmgg> License <http://creativecommons.org/licenses/by-sa/3.0/deed.en>

p.7 Creative Commons <http://tinyurl.com/mrfprjv> This photo has been modified: its original is in colour.

p.11 Public Domain <http://tinyurl.com/o4r5r87>

p.12 Public Domain < http://tinyurl.com/n9jjt6t >

p.15 Public Domain <http://tinyurl.com/m97f3th>

p.18 Public Domain <http://tinyurl.com/kpmjmag>

p.18 Public Domain <http://tinyurl.com/lofmj2v>

p.19 Public Domain <http://tinyurl.com/mbb8c6w>

p.21 Public Domain <http://tinyurl.com/ltqbu89>

p.22 Public Domain http://tinyurl.com/kn2awc3

p.23 Public Domain <http://tinyurl.com/q3toyjw>

p.24 Public Domain <http://tinyurl.com/me7zmkv>

p.26 Public Domain <http://tinyurl.com/q5avqem>

p.26 Public Domain <http://en.wikipedia.org/wiki/Doukhobor>

p.30 Public Domain <http://tinyurl.com/oh26t4k>

p.30 Public Domain <http://tinyurl.com/prukz77>

p.33 Creative Commons <http://tinyurl.com/n9prggz>

p.33 Public Domain <http://tinyurl.com/p5jwg23>

The Mocking Serenade

p.36 Public Domain <http://tinyurl.com/lcxbqez>

p.38 Photo by the author

p.39 Public Domain Photograph of students from Fort Albany Residential School reading in class overseen by a nun c 1945. From the Edmund Metatawabin collection at the University of Algoma <http://tinyurl.com/m84ffmg>

p.41 Public Domain <http://tinyurl.com/obtm4nl>

p.42 Public Domain <http://tinyurl.com/pq35gah>

p.45 Public Domain <http://tinyurl.com/lqyx985>

p.46 Public Domain <http://tinyurl.com/llufqrq>

p.48 Public Domain <http://tinyurl.com/m6ds59j>

p.51 Creative Commons <http://tinyurl.com/jvzqr3a> This photo has been modified: the original is in colour.

p.52 Creative Commons <http://tinyurl.com/lmty3k6> This photo has been modified: the original is in colour.

p.52 Creative Commons <http://tinyurl.com/m5mjj96> and <http://tinyurl.com/k6jxkjz> These photos have been modified: their originals are in colour.

p.52 Creative Commons <http://tinyurl.com/k6jxkjz> This photo has been modified: the original is in colour.

p. 54 Creative Commons < http://tinyurl.com/orygn47 >

p.56 Public Domain <http://en.wikipedia.org/wiki/Situationist_International>

p.59 Public Domain <http://tinyurl.com/nh8q3af>

p.61 Creative Commons <http://tinyurl.com/q3yqe4s>

p.63 Public Domain <http://tinyurl.com/oa2n8u5>

p.64 Creative Commons <http://tinyurl.com/qhbo969>

Illustrations

p.70 Public Domain <http://tinyurl.com/dylmg3j

p. 74 Benoit Rochon, Creative Commons http://tinyurl.com/q9cdca4 This photo has been modified: the original is in colour.

ⓘ	Attribution <creativecommons.org/licenses/by-sa/2.0/deed.en>
ⓢ	ShareAlike <http://creativecommons.org/licenses/by-sa/3.0/deed.en>
Ⓢ	Public Domain
Ⓞ	No Rights Reserved http://creativecommons.org/about/cc0
ⓒⓒ	Creative Commons http://creativecommons.org

CHARIVARI PRESS
ANNOUNCES
SCARLET LETTER #5

LEAVING NO MARK:
PROLEGOMENA TO AN EVANESCENT ART

BY DONAL MCGRAITH

978-1-895166-40-8 • $10.95 • £7.95 • 97 pages • paperbound
Worldwide release, June 15, 2015.

"Art is fakery, a lie," begins *Leaving No Mark: Prolegomena to an Evanescent Art*. In this striking essay, one by one, Donal McGraith dismantles our fundamental assumptions about Western art; especially that it consists of static works of originality and rare genius. Such views of art, as a specialized activity, are the basis for its academic study and the foundation of the multi-billion dollar art market. In particular in discussing, copies, fakes and reproductions he destroys the foundation for aesthetic uniqueness. This fallacy has given rise to a "cult of personality" and a "prison house of style," whose only purpose to inflate the art market. The so-called original operates in a similar mystifying way to the religious relic, the value lies less in aesthetic quality but only in the notion, more often untrue as fakes abound, that the 'genius' has touched the object.

McGraith seeks to reclaim art as the lived expression of our creativity urging that we not direct these impulses into forms that can be quickly turned into commodities. Like Navajo sand painting or the ceilidh, such endeavours would soon be lost to time. Other strategies supporting an evanescent approach are developed in a section entitled, "Anonymity, Pseudonymity & Polynymity."

Donal McGraith is the author of *The Wild and the Free: Shane, Rousseau, Hippies*. also published by Charivari Press. He has produced a number of articles on music and art for the magazines *Musicworks* and *Sub Rosa*. His seminal essay 'Anti-Copyright and Cassette Culture' was included in *Sound By Artists*. McGraith's provocative views, unsettling to those who benefit from high art, are clearly on display in *Leaving No Mark*.

www.charivaripress.com
CHARIVARI PRESS

ALSO FROM THIS SERIES
SCARLET LETTER #3

THE WILD AND THE FREE:
SHANE, ROUSSEAU, HIPPIES

BY DONAL MCGRAITH

978-1-895166-32-3 • $10.95 • £7.95 • 97 pages • paperbound

The Wild & The Free begins as a series of meditations about wilderness and freedom; about the American frontier in fact and fiction, and its promise of freedom for refugees. But then it draws back to consider Rousseau, Zerzan and the largely negative effects on humanity and personal freedom which stem from the advent of agriculture. Along the way, Donal McGraith considers such topics as 'buyer's regret,' which is evidenced by our consumerism and attempts to convince ourselves that we have not lost something of value. And he takes a detailed look at the film Shane whose chief protagonist exemplifies the impossibility of personal integrity when faced by the demands of loyalty brought about by civilization. With his insistence on individual responsibility, Shane chooses to become an outsider, to stand apart from the family, law and gangs that compete for his allegiance.

Part screed, McGraith attacks the complicity between post-modernism, technocracy and consumerism. His criticism of our complacency with misery, homelessness, and ecological disaster is ruthless. Distracted by the pursuit of things, he demonstrates our complicity in global misery. Wholesale capitulation to so-called technological innovation has allowed us to ignore the utter degradation and self-loathing we incarnate. McGraith finds clues to a different kind of life we all know to be possible which utterly condemns our moral vacancy. Filled with provocative insights, this is a personal and unconventional book.

Donal McGraith has produced a number of articles on music and art for the magazines *Musicworks* and *Sub Rosa*. His seminal essay 'Anti-Copyright and Cassette Culture' was included in *Sound By Artists*. McGraith's provocative views, unsettling to those who benefit from high art, are clearly on display in *Leaving No Mark*.

www.charivaripress.com
CHARIVARI PRESS

Also From by Rod Dubey

Scarlet letter #2

...Beautiful in my worn clothes...
The Transgressions of Love

978-1-895166-10-1 • $10.95 • £7.95 • 89 pages • paperbound

...beautiful in my worn clothes...The Transgressions of Love is an essay on the transgressive nature of love. Love is described as a river that freely flows without regard to prohibitions based on race, gender, class or religion. It transgresses the boundaries set by church, state and family which seek to control it and is thus, inherently subversive. From the moment we begin to love those outside of our family we are on a path which undermines its power over our lives.

Scarlet letter #1

Indecent Acts in a Public Place:
Sports, Insolence & Sedition

978-1-895166-00-2 • $10.95 • £7.95 • 78 pages • paperbound

In its four striking essays, Rod Dubey challenges the idea that sport indoctrinates men into being good corporate citizens. Sports teams are seen as a form of men's society that excludes and subjugates women while challenging day-to-day morality. Like the gang, teams defend a territory and resist corporate control with their own nebulous power structure. Sports are a reflection of shifting definitions of masculinity and also, for the viewer, provide the opportunity for an active gaze where male fantasies are played out.

www.charivaripress.com
Charivari Press

www.ingramcontent.com/pod-product-compliance
Lightning Source LLC
LaVergne TN
LVHW041538060526
838200LV00037B/1041